Praise for

Intimate Conversations with the Divine

'I've loved so many of Caroline Myss' books, but maybe none so much as *Intimate Conversations with the Divine*. Has there ever been a more urgent need for her unique and profound (and sometimes wonderfully cranky) take on our spiritual reality, healing and the language of holiness? These invocations of grace, her guidance and her own innermost prayers, are medicine for our souls during these tumultuous times.'

— **Anne Lamott**, *New York Times* bestselling author of *Hallelujah Anyway* and *Help, Thanks, Wow*

'*Intimate Conversations with the Divine* shows us that prayer isn't some esoteric activity reserved for a holy few; it's a language we are born knowing. These pages will encourage anyone who has lost the habit of daily prayer to take it up again, and inspire anyone who has never prayed to start the conversation now.'

— **Maria Shriver**, bestselling author and award-winning journalist

'Caroline Myss has written a book that sets the power of Prayer free from the monastery, allowing it to enter our hearts and minds as an essential Grace for these challenging modern times. In re-envisioning how we dialogue with the Divine, Caroline's profound, clear spiritual direction offers new direct access to Prayer's healing power and enduring capacity to help us up any mountain that we've been called to climb. New soulful summits of your life's potential await you through *Intimate Conversations with the Divine*.'

— **Robert Ohotto**, intuitive strategist and bestselling author of *Transforming Fate into Destiny*

'These heartfelt conversations with the divine offer a profound invitation to express our own spiritual questions and concerns, yearnings and deepest dreams. With the warmth and wisdom of a good friend, Caroline Myss has given us a treasure trove of spiritual insight for these troubled times.'

— **Clark Strand and Perdita Finn**, co-authors of *The Way of the Rose: The Radical Path of the Divine Feminine Hidden in the Rosary*

'What is the prayer you most need to pray in your life? Do you know how it begins? In *Intimate Conversations with the Divine*, Caroline Myss teaches you a whole new way to pray. Praying with God, not to God. Filled with 100 beautiful prayers – holy moments of divine intimacy – this mystical handbook helps you cultivate a practice of daily deep prayer that invites a whole new level of guidance, grace and inspiration into your life.'

— **Robert Holden**, author of *Holy Shift!* and *Finding Love Everywhere*

'In this book Caroline Myss invites us to listen in as she prays to the Lord her God. As we listen, we realize she is encouraging us to speak to the Lord Our God of all the expected and unexpected things our heart wants us to say. And, as our own voice falls silent, to then listen to the still small voice of God that is always there guiding and sustaining us in each passing moment of our lives.'

— **James Finley**, Contemplative Teacher with the Center for Action and Contemplation

'Once again, Caroline Myss lights the way, showing us how the epidemics of this time must ultimately be addressed at the level of the soul... This is prayer with power and energy – the power to breathe and instill life; the energy of unconditional love that opens us up so that we once again feel that which most nourishes and ultimately heals.'

— **Dr Jeffrey Rediger**, Harvard Medical School, author of *Cured: The New Science of Spontaneous Healing*

'In *A Course in Miracles* it's written that "prayer is the medium of miracles." At no time in the world has it been more obvious that humanity is in need of power that we alone cannot bestow. Caroline Myss presents the most ancient of powers in a startlingly relevant way.'

— **Marianne Williamson**, author

'Caroline Myss beautifully succeeds in awakening the lost language of prayer, a holy language that our world needs as never before. Her prayers are flashes of her intimacies with the divine... It is always brave to share the intimacy of the messages hidden in silence. When this courage is matched by true gentleness, the effect is powerful healing; her prayers will heal sick souls. Caroline's evident care for others and her spirit of service will make this book a true friend and companion for those in need at every step of their life's journey.'

— **Laurence Freeman**, Benedictine monk and leader of
the World Community for Christian Meditation

'Every thought is a prayer. Thinking sets in motion spiritual forces to create change. *Intimate Conversations with the Divine* provides that essential thinking for the optimal mystical life.'

— **Dr C Norman Shealy**, president of Shealy-Sorin Wellness and Holos
Energy Medicine Education

'At a time when we need to reawaken our relationship with the Divine, along comes *Intimate Conversations with the Divine*, which spoke deep inside the heart of my longings, visions and truths. This book will awaken anyone who is asleep, and to those who are awakened, it will add more fuel to your "awakeness." The whole world needs to deepen their conversations with the Divine, and Caroline's new book will take you to a place to find all of your life's solutions. The best read I have come across in decades!'

— **Sister Dr Jenna**, Brahma Kumaris, radio host,
America Meditating

'Sometimes I feel as if I go through the day barely able to see, unable to hear, saying things I don't really mean. A lost human being in a sea of other stressed-out, disconnected people. What to do? I'll tell you what to do: read this book! It clears a path through the dark woods of our times. Caroline Myss says that the true meaning of prayer is a request for help in how to see. Reading *Intimate Conversations with the Divine* gave me new sight, opened my ears and helped me say beautiful, meaningful, powerful new prayers.'

— **Elizabeth Lesser**, co-founder of Omega Institute, author of *Broken Open* and *Cassandra Speaks*

'In this honest and unique spiritual diary, Caroline Myss invites us to a daring journey into the inner truth of our deepest selves... Myss shares with us a deeply personal glimpse into her own mystical soul and – if we listen deeply – into our own... In a time of religious deconstruction, Myss dares to reconstruct. She calls us to the deeper meaning and practice of prayer – one that will serve us well in these challenging times.'

— **Matthew Fox**, author of *Prayer: A Radical Response to Life*, *The Tao of Thomas Aquinas* and *Naming the Unnameable*

'Open this book and be astonished. It is at once a revelation and a spirit-quaking reminder of the power and practice of prayer. It is also the Passion Play of a mystic, Caroline Myss, as she daily enters into spirited conversation with the Divine, receiving insights that are as welcome as finding cool spring water in the desert. Soul deep and winsomely wise, Caroline brooks no whiny naysaying but persists in her talks until the laughter of God brings fresh insights, potent knowings into our human space and time. But be warned. You cannot commune with this book without being changed and charged. For you come to discover that you not only live in the sacred cosmos but that it also lives in you. We are One Holy System. And then the great duet begins!'

— **Jean Houston, PhD**, Chancellor of Meridian University, author of *The Wizard of Us* and *The Search for the Beloved*

'The power of prayer is resurfacing in our collective consciousness right at the moment we are all experiencing the shattering effects of the pandemic together. Right at the moment we are all in the same conversation about our vulnerabilities and concerns about the future, we are realizing that we need, once again, to pray. Caroline has shared a pathway of prayers back to the Divine. Only prayer can lead us now.'

— **Jim Garrison**, PhD, President of Ubiquity University

'Caroline is giving all of us exactly what we need to nourish our courage and embolden our embattled hope – a book on prayer that is not only a mystical classic but direct guidance as to how to align, nakedly and passionately, with the Divine from the most authentic part of ourselves. This book is far more than a masterpiece – it is a blazing manifesto of Truth and Empowerment which no sincere lover of God can afford not to read, learn from and integrate profoundly.'

— **Andrew Harvey**, author of *The Hope: A Guide to Sacred Activism* and, with Carolyn Baker, *Savage Grace: How to Live Resiliently in the Global Dark Night*

'I inhaled this book—a very personal and powerful prayer journey that is a gift to us all. The importance of holy language is critical, now more than ever. The perfect read for anyone who needs a boost of much-needed grace.'

—**Jenniffer Weigel**, Emmy Award–winning journalist, author of *This Isn't the Life I Ordered* and *I'm Spiritual, Dammit!*

'In this luminous collection of sacred conversations, Caroline Myss reclaims holy language and offers it back as blessing, as birthright, as a lighthouse beckoning us home from the storms of the human condition. Each prayer is drenched with potency, richly wrought, simultaneously particular and universal. What a gift to be invited to listen in on the intimate conversations between a master teacher and her God, and to find here the possibility of a direct response to our own innermost yearnings.'

— **Mirabai Starr**, translator of Teresa of Avila and John of the Cross, author of *God of Love* and *Wild Mercy*

'When Caroline Myss asked me to review her book *Intimate Conversations with the Divine*, I was unprepared for what I was in for. On the surface her book is about how prayer is the sacred language through which we intimately connect with something beyond and greater than ourselves. While reading her words, however, I was shocked – and delighted – when I began having the experience that something alive was speaking to me, as if I was in dialogue with another part of myself. But even more than that, in reading her book I began to intuitively feel through my heart that her words weren't about prayer, but were, in a very magical and unexpected way, answering a prayer of mine. It was as if a deeper part of myself had dreamed up Caroline's book to come my way at exactly the right moment in time in order to remind me how to deepen my communion with my own soul. I can't recommend *Intimate Conversations with the Divine* highly enough. Caroline has offered us a true gift that couldn't be more needed at this time in our history.'

— **Paul Levy**, author of *Dispelling Wetiko* and *The Quantum Revelation*

'These prayers help us name our longings and give us permission to show up before God with new honesty and vulnerability. They encourage us to listen to those almost-silent whispers of God, who – like a gentle mother – is always eager to embrace us in our brokenness and bring us closer to Her heart. . . . Giving voice to these prayers will change you and empower you to be the healing presence our world needs right now.'

— **Fr Adam Bucko**, co-author of *Occupy Spirituality* and *The New Monasticism* and director of The Center for Spiritual Imagination at the Cathedral of the Incarnation in New York

Intimate Conversations with the Divine

ALSO BY CAROLINE MYSS

Anatomy of the Spirit
Archetypes*
The Creation of Health
Defy Gravity*
Entering the Castle
Invisible Acts of Power
Sacred Contracts
Why People Don't Heal
and How They Can

*Available from Hay House

Please visit:

Hay House UK: www.hayhouse.co.uk
Hay House USA: www.hayhouse.com®
Hay House Australia: www.hayhouse.com.au
Hay House India: www.hayhouse.co.in

***

Intimate Conversations with the Divine

with the Divine

PRAYER, GUIDANCE, and GRACE

CAROLINE MYSS

HAY HOUSE

HAY HOUSE
Carlsbad, California • New York City
London • Sydney • New Delhi

Published in the United Kingdom by:
Hay House UK Ltd, The Sixth Floor, Watson House,
54 Baker Street, London W1U 7BU
Tel: +44 (0)20 3927 7290; Fax: +44 (0)20 3927 7291; www.hayhouse.co.uk

Published in the United States of America by:
Hay House Inc., PO Box 5100, Carlsbad, CA 92018-5100
Tel: (1) 760 431 7695 or (800) 654 5126
Fax: (1) 760 431 6948 or (800) 650 5115; www.hayhouse.com

Published in Australia by:
Hay House Australia Ltd, 18/36 Ralph St, Alexandria NSW 2015
Tel: (61) 2 9669 4299; Fax: (61) 2 9669 4144; www.hayhouse.com.au

Published in India by:
Hay House Publishers India, Muskaan Complex, Plot No.3, B-2,
Vasant Kunj, New Delhi 110 070
Tel: (91) 11 4176 1620; Fax: (91) 11 4176 1630; www.hayhouse.co.in

Cover design: Rae Myss and Ploy Siripant
Interior design: Bryn Starr Best

The information given in this book should not be treated as a substitute for professional medical advice; always consult a medical practitioner. Any use of information in this book is at the reader's discretion and risk. Neither the author nor the publisher can be held responsible for any loss, claim or damage arising out of the use, or misuse, of the suggestions made, the failure to take medical advice or for any material on third-party websites.

A catalogue record for this book is available from the British Library.

Tradepaper ISBN: 978-1-78180-147-5
E-book ISBN: 978-1-4019-5256-3
Audiobook ISBN: 978-1-4019-2292-4

Printed and bound in Great Britain by
TJ Books Limited, Padstow, Cornwall

*Dedicated to the power
of grace and prayer*

Contents

Preface

As this book prepares to go to press, and for the first time in the history of humanity, all of us everywhere are whirling together in a cyclone of transformation. Only the Divine could orchestrate such chaos. And though scientists are looking for—and will eventually track down—the physical genesis of the virus we are battling as I write this, the handiwork of the Divine is clearly behind it. The source of this chaos is organic: a microbe. It is not political, and it is not a war. Because it is organic and global, we are all in this together. We are *meant* to be in this together because we are *meant* to undergo a vast, profound shift of consciousness—together.

This is not the first pandemic we've seen. We have been living in a psychic pandemic of fear for many years: fear of other people and other religions, fear of not having enough, fear of nuclear war. What have we not feared? Our entire consciousness has been waiting for the crisis ball to drop, and now it has.

The great spiritual masters held as their core holy truth that we are all one living, breathing soul. Any other view of reality was a distraction, an illusion, a prop in the theater of the physical world. What was immortal about us—our soul—was born knowing this truth. And elusive as it was, this truth would pulsate within us throughout our lives, causing us to continually search for that greater "something else" we knew must be operating behind the scenes. We would not stop this quest until we finally looked within and discovered the realm of the sacred—inside ourselves.

I believe we are emerging into the organic era of the Divine: the era when we will finally recognize that the laws of mysticism and nature are coded into our blood and bones. In the decades ahead, human beings will evolve beyond the religions that divide us and engage more fully—more consciously—with the mystical laws of co-creation. We have spent the decades since the 1960s learning—through countless paths, from self-healing to self-empowerment, from meditation and yoga to quantum physics—that we co-create our reality, individually and collectively. Now we must weave that powerful truth consciously and lovingly with each other. We are the engines of all that happens on this Earth. *We* are. That realization is the core truth of an organic understanding of the Divine, of the holy cosmic Light that breathes with all creation. The Divine is *all creation*. Nothing exists outside this holy light. All is creation, and all creation is conscious. Look up, sideways, or within and you will never see anything outside the nature and power of the Divine.

I converse with this God of life all the time. In prayer I share my thoughts, my problems, my dilemmas, and my musings. I have learned to attune my inner world to the subtle nature of heaven: the way it whispers and guides us, the way it waits until we are ready to respond, the way it blocks us from our own foolishness, and the way it lets us create our own mistakes or become masters of our own genius. The message in the current transformative chaos is that it is time for us to understand the nature of the Divine—manifested within all creation, breathing through all life, and expressed in the laws that govern the mystical realm, the material realm, and yes, even the health of our physical bodies. We are one holy system of life and great cosmic truth, which is that all life—including all of us—breathes together. I hope this book, these prayers, will bring you comfort and grace, and help you through the difficult times ahead. And I hope they will inspire you to believe that with God, all things are possible: endless miracles, divine intervention, and the intimate company of holy angels.

Love,

Caroline Myss
Oak Park, Illinois
March 2020

Introduction

The Power of Prayer

From the first time human beings looked up at the heavens and wondered about creation to the first sound hummed in cosmic awe to the first time we danced around a fire, painted images of power beings on cave walls, or sacrificed animals—and even other people—something in us sensed that nature, the source of all life, was conscious. It was conscious, and it was listening. When have we not prayed?

Yet even as prayer is our primal language, it is also a lost language. Through the centuries the ways people worship—the gods we pray to, and how we conceptualize god—have changed. Our experience of God is evolving past the half-man, half-god myths of the Abrahamic traditions. The power of the Divine is, and always has been, *pure power,* transcendent of human imagery. But it's only since the middle of the last century that we humans have begun to see past those old images in any significant way. The result is that we are living in a transition, releasing the mythologies of the past and evolving into a new myth, one capable of relating to the psyches and souls of a changing global community. I believe this shift heralds a great turning point in our evolution, one far greater than we can comprehend. At the core of this transformation is our collective awakening to the power of our soul, to our mystical nature, and to a mystically organic understanding of the nature of the Divine.

And yet in this transition something has been lost—and we are suffering for it. We've removed holy language from our common parlance and the act of prayer from our daily lives. Prayer has assisted humans in the navigation of life for millennia because a direct connection to the Divine is essential in navigating life's challenges. Yet how many of us call upon that connection in our everyday lives? Too few of us understand how this connection—or lack thereof—influences our thinking, decision making, and even our health. Too few of us understand that without the grace that is carried by sacred language, our souls will literally starve.

Our disconnection from the holy language of prayer may well be a contributing factor, if not the deepest soul reason, for the epidemics we are now experiencing: depression, anxiety, and relationship crises, as well as the breakdown in ethical and moral reasoning in our society. For the yearning to be connected to the Divine does not go away just because our cultural myths have become outdated. Myths are stories that tell of our relationship to the sacred, of our *need* for the sacred, of the truth that we are governed by sacred law. The passing of the religious era signals the need for a *change in*—not a phasing out of—our personal, intimate relationship to the laws of the Universe.

The childhood story "The Princess and the Pea" comes to mind. The princess kept stacking mattresses on top of a small pea, yet she could still feel it, which prevented her from sleeping. That pea is our holy interior. We've done our best to cover it over, forget about it, partly deliberately and partly out of ignorance of its essential role in our well-being. Yet the sacred still calls to us. We will never feel quite right, never quite at peace, until we are communicating with our own soul, and the cosmos, regularly. At the end of the day, we are sacred beings. We forget that at great peril to ourselves.

We are built for belief. Belief shapes the way we see divine power and our role within it. This is the first time in the history of humanity when the majority of people do not know what they believe in. Do you understand how unprecedented this is? It is a phenomenon that has never existed before, so most of us don't realize the psychic trauma it puts us through. And what it opens us up to, how vulnerable we have become. Words are vessels, and they can be filled with either light—or its opposite. Both can be equally compelling. When we do not know what we believe in—when we do not feel empowered to have an intimate, personal, conversational relationship with God—we are susceptible to believing the most potent voice in the room. And sometimes that voice comes carrying a darkness unimaginable. It takes a lot of light, a lot of faith, to sustain yourself around the kind of darkness that appears in the vacuum of religion. You have to sustain a field of grace around you, which comes from being mindful of what you believe in. Mindful and prayerful.

Every word we say has the capacity to hurt or heal. To lift someone out of darkness or to plunge them into despair. This is the power of language. Recognizing that we hold this power is what it means to become conscious. For we indeed co-create our reality, right down to the micro level. The tool God gave us for this effort is *language*. Each word we speak is a brick we lay, building the world we live in. How am I going to speak about this experience? Is it a "crisis" or an "opportunity"? A "blessing" or a "catastrophe"? Words are vessels for light; they are how we exercise our mystical and creative power. They are literally the expression of God pouring through us. The proof that God hears everything is found in the ability to create and destroy with our words. Just as words can be made holy through sincerity, they can be weaponized through negative intent. This is the great gift and also the profound responsibility of being on a spiritual journey today.

So perhaps you can begin to see the importance of prayer. When we pray, we ask the Divine to show us how to see, how to speak, how to create. We ask God to reveal, to illuminate, the right path for us. *God, show me how to see this. Reveal your wisdom to me, Lord. Show me the way. One word will do. One word is all I need.* Then, suddenly, the word *hope* arises in you. Or *patience*. This word, this revelation, becomes the most holy word you have. You can hang on to it; you can use it to guide you. This is the true meaning of prayer: a request for help in how to see.

This is why I had to write this book, to urge you toward this new way to pray, one that is not about supplication and asking God to remove the consequences of your bad decisions. It's not to explain why bad things happen to good people—that's above my pay grade. It's to share my way of prayer, which is a simple request for grace. "Help me out here, God. Don't let me say something stupid. Give me the words. If I try to do this on my own, I'm going to do damage."

Words are like a knife, a tool that can be incredibly useful when correctly applied but easy to mishandle. And the results can be fatal. When you pray, you're asking God to help you pick up the knife by the handle. If you don't have that open channel of communication with the Divine, you're likely to pick it up by the blade and cut your hand open. Or worse, use it to harm someone else. Prayer is a request for help in using the tool you've been given wisely. You're saying, "I know language is a tool, Lord, but I am not always trustworthy with how I use it. If I do this my way, I'm bound to harm someone. I need your help." When you die, God's going to say, "What did you do with the tool I gave you? I gave you a great tool. You could have built a city or a world with it. You needed to ask me how to use it. But you didn't ask."

Prayer is how you ask. If you start with prayer, you'll always end up holding the knife by the handle, not the blade. It's as simple as that.

THE MYSTICAL LIFE OPENS

Years ago, I would never have considered writing on or about prayer. I am someone who believed for a long time, as perhaps you have too, that a person's spiritual practice—or lack of one—is that person's business. I believe that my spiritual life, my soul life, is a part of my *private* life rather than my professional life. That creed served me for 35 years in my career as a medical intuitive and teacher. My focus during those years was on identifying illness, creating the template for the human energy system, and eventually studying the power and influence of archetypal patterns. I was more than happy to leave soul matters on the sidelines.

During those years of my career, I had no interest in what someone believed or did not believe. Connecting people to the Divine, and to their own soul, was not my job. My job was to teach students about energy anatomy, guide them to access their intuition, and uncover their sacred archetypes. I was interested in matters of the mind and body, and did not feel it was my place to talk about the soul.

Then, about 15 years ago, my spiritual journey unexpectedly collided with my professional life. None of us is ever prepared for these detours that come out of nowhere, and I am no exception. It happened on a lovely, quiet, nearly perfect October afternoon. I was standing in the kitchen of my townhouse, musing about how good I was feeling and how much I genuinely loved my life. I was like someone eating goodie-blessings off a conveyor belt, each one inflating my state of happiness and contentment just a little bit more. *Could I ever be more content or happy?* I wondered.

All of a sudden—out of nowhere and related to absolutely nothing that I was thinking—I heard a voice from within say, "You do not have a prayer life."

"What?" I said out loud, as if I had just been asked a question by someone standing in my kitchen.

Again, I heard this soft whisper saying, "You do not have a prayer life."

Then—and you have to picture this—I actually began speaking out loud. To . . . whom? I didn't know. But I felt I had to plead my case, justify my lack of attention to a prayer life.

I said, "Well, I teach on spirituality and I study sacred literature all the time. And, hey, I do all those medical intuitive readings."

And then I stopped. *What was I doing? To whom was I speaking?*

A fear locked ahold of me. I stood frozen, silent, barely breathing. I wanted to tell myself that I had just imagined that micro-mystical experience so I did not have to acknowledge the significance of the message. Unfortunately, I *had* gotten the message. And it was not just about praying. That inner voice left sacred residue inside me. In a mystical microsecond, that presence had communicated a sensation of familiarity, of purpose, of intimate watchfulness. The presence radiated power unlike anything I had ever felt on my own.

I kept replaying the moment over and over again in my thoughts. As the days passed, my immediate response of fear was replaced by unrestrained awe. I began to dwell in the thought that somehow, and for some reason, my life was in need of prayer. Not only that, but somehow I needed to be informed about it. The thought astounded me. *Who pays that much attention to each of us? How is it possible that we are so carefully watched?* One always goes to the opposite position as well, wondering how others did *not* receive such guidance before accidents or murders. How can you not wonder about those logical questions? But there are no logical answers when it comes to mystical matters—none at all. These experiences are what they are. Mystical experiences are not meant to put bad things right with the world or explain why painful things happen. Mystical experiences are soul directed and soul driven. They are not involved with or attached to the grime and grit of daily human life. They are transcendent. They transform us, and we in turn transform life.

I knew that my whole life had just changed because of that micro-mystical experience. I would certainly begin a deeper prayer life, but I had not gotten that message simply because I needed to spend another 10 minutes a day in prayer. I was being called to an entirely new path. I wasn't sure about the details; I only knew without the slightest doubt that the needle on my compass had shifted. I was meant to explore the territory of the soul. And it would *require* a prayer life. And that was that.

CHANNELING GRACE

From that point onward, my inner habits began to shift. I needed more time alone. I gradually lost my enthusiasm for teaching about archetypes and sacred contracts, subjects I had adored and taught for nearly 15 years. In workshops I went from observing patterns in my students—like the archetype of the Wounded Child or the Rescuer—to noticing who in the room seemed to be the most vulnerable. I started to snoop, asking the students how they were feeling, what their inner lives were like. I couldn't get over how much I genuinely cared about their responses.

The 15 years of my life since have been devoted to deepening my understanding of contemporary mystical consciousness, of the soul and its expressions. I turned my attention toward teaching on the great mystics: the Catholics—St. John of the Cross, Ignatius of Loyola, and Teresa of Ávila—as well as Rumi and Khalil Gibran of the Eastern traditions. St. Teresa in particular captured my attention, quite literally interrupting me onstage during a teaching with the simple imperative "Daughter, follow me." I did, and made exploring her teachings the subject of my next book, *Entering the Castle.*

They say that when the student is ready, the teacher appears. For me, that was Teresa, and as you will see, her influence shows up in my prayers—and in the pages of this book. But it turns out that the converse is also true: when the *teacher* is ready, the students appear. And so they did. I began to present workshops on healing, spirituality, and mysticism—all subjects of the soul rather than merely the spirit. The classes filled immediately with people coping with every type of suffering, from terminal illness to chronic physical pain to depression. I should have felt out of my league, but I did not feel the least bit overwhelmed. Instead I had an ever-present thought, an active spark of grace, that my role was to teach about the soul—and heaven's role was to heal. I truly got it.

Since that time I have met countless individuals who were encountering profound soul crises with little guidance as to how to cope. You yourself may be wondering whether you have had—or are now experiencing—a similar crisis. You have come to the right place, for once I turned my attention to all matters related to the soul, many of the mysteries that had stirred in me over the years found answers. I discovered that problems of the soul cannot be addressed by energy work or even archetypes. They must be addressed at the level of the soul. Just as physical disease may require medicine to heal, so a soul crisis requires its own medicine. That medicine is grace, administered via intimate, personal connection to the Divine through prayer.

Perhaps it is obvious that the same laws governing all of nature govern our biology and anatomy. But do you realize that at the level of the soul, these same principles are the *mystical* laws? God *is* law. Law has no religion. Law is consistent. Law and order are universal manifestations of the nature of the Divine—impersonal, systematic, integrated, and built into all systems of life, from the natural world to the nature of your very soul.

This is where prayer comes in. Where it becomes an absolute requirement. Because in keeping with the paradoxical nature of the Divine, this vast, sacred, living, breathing, holy cosmos is also very intimate; for we each reside within the nature of God. And the bridge between this impersonal, cosmic system and each one of us is prayer. Prayer is how we communicate with the cosmos; it is the means through which we make ourselves known and heard in the vastness of space. And it's how we receive guidance in return. Prayer is our channel of communication, the direct line between the soul and the Divine. We are built for this divine intimacy—and for the awe, belief, and inspiration it creates.

The experience of awe—of believing that something greater than ourselves is present and somehow involved with this human experience—is a constant in our fundamental nature, as critical to our sense of well-being as food and water. An experience of awe can inspire us to "rise from the dead," to climb out of the darkness of depression and despair. It is the hidden force behind health and healing, the genesis of every observable miracle. Similarly the graces of faith, hope, trust, inner counsel, endurance, and fortitude, among so many others, soothe our souls unlike any other force.

Yet here we are, living in a crisis of faith. We have become distanced from our own souls, from belief in anything beyond what we can see. We cannot survive living such soulless lives. Just look at the consequences; look at what we have created. We split the atom, and suddenly we are capable of killing millions of our fellow human beings with the touch of a button. Think of the power we have given ourselves. We are literally burning alive from climate change, and we've decided that maybe there's not even a god!

This is the era when we will either wake up in terms of our inner lives or we will pay a serious price. I deeply believe that.

We need to learn to speak to God intimately, directly, and often. We can no longer pray *to* God; we must pray *with* God. And we must pray *with* and *for* each other. This book, a collection of my own personal prayers, a prayer journal of sorts, is my contribution to that effort. I hope that through these prayers you will come to understand the role prayer has to play in reconnecting you—and us—to our own souls, to awe, and to divine grace. I hope it will inspire you to make the practice of speaking directly to a cosmic God the heart of your spiritual life. Returning prayer to where it belongs: the very center of our world.

HOW TO USE THIS BOOK

I never imagined myself sharing these intimate prayers with the world. But as my teaching evolved over the past decade, I realized many of my students were at a loss when it came to prayer. They did not understand its importance or that it still had an essential role to play. So I began reading my prayers at the end of each session I taught. Without fail, students would approach me during breaks, asking where they could get copies of the prayers. *Copies of my own personal dialogues?* I thought. *Why would anybody want that?* But the requests came so often, and so consistently, that eventually I gave in. So this is what you will find in the pages that follow: my intimate, one-on-one dialogues with God.

My form of prayer may strike some people as radical: I converse directly with God. I always have. And it has never occurred to me that my prayers are not heard, though I know they read as if I am talking to myself. But I am not, not really. I see my way of prayer as a form of mystical dialogue, an inner conversation in which I share exactly what I am thinking about, what I am

struggling with. And soon—always—an answer shows up. Sometimes one occurs to me later, while I am writing. At other times a
thought comes in completely out of the blue. It's like sending out
an e-mail to my most trusted correspondent; I *know* I will receive
an answer. I live in complete trust about the way heaven works,
and I have never been disappointed.

No one comes to a truly profound understanding of the power
of prayer except through direct experience. Yet I am aware that it
can be useful to have a road map, and that is my intention with
this book. By sharing my own intimate prayers, my dialogues with
the Divine, I hope to give you access to what I have always known
about prayer. First, that it need not be formal. It is an intimate
type of communication, as simple as having a conversation with
a friend. Second, that it opens a channel between you and the
Divine, between your individual soul and the impersonal, holy
cosmos. Through this channel, grace can flow. Finally, that you
don't need to understand *how* it works—only that it does. In fact,
releasing the need to understand is part of the process of reclaim-
ing your holy sense of awe, your belief in something much bigger
than your mind could ever understand.

Each prayer, as you will see, is an invocation of the grace I
needed on that particular day. To help illuminate my intention for
each prayer, I've followed each prayer with a "guidance" or teaching that explores the themes of that particular dialogue, of the
grace it is meant to call in. And I've included a direct invocation
of that grace, which you may use as you find your way toward your
own path of prayer.

If you already know which grace your soul needs today, you
may turn to the index on page 267 and search for a prayer that
speaks directly to it. Alternatively, you may use this book as a
guide of sorts, intuitively turning to a particular page and partak-
ing of whichever grace you find there.

A Word on Religion

You will notice that I refer to God as "Lord," which is a holdover from my Catholic upbringing. Some things just stick in our spiritual DNA. But I no longer adhere to any image of the Divine that looks remotely like "us." It is my understanding that God expresses "itself" through the cosmic law and order of nature—both around us and within us. When people tell me they do not believe in God, I often think I would not believe in the God they have in their heads either. But those images and ideas are not God. They are the scar tissue of bad experiences and outdated mythologies, and a mess of whatever else. We have a history of difficult marriages and divorces in our society, don't we? Most of the people I meet carry wounds from their childhoods, which are products of bad marriages that included incest and brutality, adultery and abuse. And yet do we toss out our search for romantic love because of the sins committed in human marriages? Hardly. We cannot stop ourselves from searching for love because we are *built* for love. We crave it.

And we crave the sacred as well, in spite of the ways human beings have mismanaged our religious organizations. We cannot throw the baby out with the bathwater; we cannot sacrifice faith in the unseen because of the perpetrations of human beings. We *need* grace. We require it. We need to be in touch with the sacred. We need to know that a power far greater than our individual selves is in charge. We need this to survive, to flourish, and to be sustained. It is not optional.

If there is one thing I could communicate to you with this book, it's that our holy channel of communication with the Divine has nothing to do with religion. Heaven is not the formal organization that religion is. Leave all the formalities in your rearview mirror. And don't let the misdeeds human beings have perpetrated in the name of religion stand in the way of your nourishing yourself with the grace of the Divine. Choose an intimate way of addressing the Divine in your prayers, one that works for you, and pray. If there's one thing I know, it's that all prayers are heard and heaven always responds.

As Teresa of Ávila observed, the interior castle can only be entered through prayer. Discussing your ideas about what you *think* God is or isn't won't work any more than talking about buying an airline ticket will get you to Europe. You have to make the decision to invest your money to buy the ticket. No investment, no trip. In the same way, accessing the soul requires a commitment to the practice of speaking directly to the Divine. It requires that you open the channel between yourself and the awe-inspiring holy cosmos, and that you allow grace to enter.

This is why it is so urgent that we re-empower ourselves into intimate conversation with God. My hope is that, ultimately, you will make use of these prayers in whatever way accomplishes that goal. Prayer reconnects your soul to the divine cosmos, and the connection is very personal. Some of my students read my prayers each night, contemplating how my words connect to their own lives. Others have used my way of prayer to inform their own, entering into a daily dialogue with the Divine on their own terms. I don't care how you use them, only that you do. For we have never needed the grace conveyed by holy language more than we need it today. It is crucial to your personal well-being, and I would daresay it's a matter of our survival as a species. Prayer is essential, it is food for the soul, and it is the one required practice of the mystical life.

My hope is that this book will help you learn to pray again. We need holy language to be active in our minds, in our hearts, and in our souls. We need faith, hope, and trust to fill us with grace, to carry us through the storms of our lives. And most of all, we need to know that we matter to life, that our life is a holy and sacred gift, that God knows us by name. And that when we pray, a light does shine upon us—that every prayer we say is heard and answered. Every single one.

100 Prayers

The pages that follow contain 100 of my own personal prayers. Many of my students use them as they are, reading and contemplating them. But truly, my intention is to inspire you to engage in a prayer practice of your own. Contemporary prayer is a dialogue with the Divine and is the conduit for grace to enter your life and our world. Each of these prayers illustrates a different type of grace that feeds the human soul. As such, I have included words of guidance as well as a petition for grace with each prayer.

1

HOW WILL YOU COME *to* ME, LORD?

Prayer

HOW WILL YOU COME TO ME, LORD? How will I know You? How will I recognize You? I know You will come for me. You will slip into my being—perhaps in the middle of the night while I sleep. Maybe You will come for me when I am not looking for You—when I am distracted, staring into an oncoming storm, fearing for my immortality. Or maybe You will come to me in the midst of a tiny lie that pours out of my mouth effortlessly. You will let me know You are listening, as I listen to myself say something that is not true as easily as if I were giving the time of day. I tell myself that small lies are insignificant. That they don't matter. How do I know what matters? How can I tell what is insignificant to my life? What if I am being tested or observed? Could I have anesthetized a part of my conscience years ago and it is You who are reawakening it now? Maybe that is how You will come to me. You will rouse my conscience out of its resting position like a sleeping dragon, one day when I am weakened by disease or fear or loneliness. And I will be forced to face the truth that I fear the many expressions of You—most of all the Light of Truth. I fear truth. You are truth itself, and I feel that power rumble like an earthquake through my being each time my eyes look into the eyes of another human being. One word of truth, exchanged through the soul portal of another, is enough to bond two human beings for eternity—a sacred union is formed. No wonder we fear truth, and yet we are compelled to seek it with every breath we take. We fear You, and cannot stop searching for You. Perhaps You will come through some truth I need to survive a calamity. You will make me need You, and I will come searching. You will make me shed my skin like a snake peeling out of a worn-out uniform. My illusions, my flaws will be exposed like boils ready for a lance. And then when I am broken, too weak to deceive even myself, there You will be—already resurrecting my soul.

Guidance

The truth is that each of us longs for some sign that heaven is watching, observing, and overseeing the journey of our life. We look for signs of God's presence in the subtle movement of the events of our lives, as we search for meaning and purpose in all we do. Though we may deny at times that we are searching for God, instead saying that we are seeking meaning and purpose, we still admit that we cannot bear the emptiness that comes from imagining that our lives are unthreaded to a sacred source. And so we wonder how, when, and in what way the Divine will come into our lives. We fear that visit as much as we search for it—because deep in our soul, we know a holy encounter is inevitable.

Grace

Lord, grant me the grace of Faith—Faith in the presence and power of You in my life. I admit to You in this quiet moment that having Faith in all matters as they unfold in my life is so very difficult. I struggle with seeing how to follow that candle on a dark night—especially when I am in the midst of chaos. And yet, I have learned that chaos is Your miracle atmosphere, spinning with the ingredients through which You work wonders. When Faith is present in me, Lord, I dwell in miracles.

Lord, hold me in the grace of Faith,
especially when my soul cannot touch its power.

2

NO SUCH THING *as* SIMPLE ACTS *of* COMPASSION

Prayer

THERE IS NO SUCH THING as a simple act of compassion or an inconsequential act of service, is there, Lord? Everything we do for another person has infinite consequences, for that person and for us. The light from stars long ago exploded can be seen in the celestial realm, traveling in all directions, with nothing to stop its journey. I believe that is the nature of our sacred light. We journey forever, even after our form implodes from exhaustion. Still, our light will continue. Particles of our light sparkle with every choice we make, every idea we have, every gift of love we share. We are living sparklers setting off eternal flames, reigniting another person's weakening ability to love, or to try again, or to get up and walk another step. There is no such thing as a small spark. When I hold that image in my head, Lord, my soul is filled with awe. We can so easily do so much for so many. It takes so very little effort to generate a spark of light from within, and it goes on forever within the soul of another human being. And so much darkness fades away. You have designed this Universe to favor the power of the light—of that I have no doubt.

Guidance

How easy it is to feel powerless, or to measure power by stuff, youth, money—the obvious substance of the material world. Those are the illusions the Buddha so aptly noted. They have no power other than the power we give them through our craving of them. And that craving costs us our real power—our soul, our light. No amount of stuff can convert into one act of compassion. But one choice made from compassion can direct endless stuff to assist the needs of so many. Which, then, is the greater power? First comes choice, the power of the soul. Choice directs our light, and compassionate choices are the ones that require the most courage of all.

Grace

Lord, there is nothing easy about praying for the grace of Compassion to reside within my heart. Compassion is a grace I would rather receive than serve as a vessel for, since then I may be asked to do more than I am truly willing to do. This grace can create consequences of the heart that I am not prepared for. And yet, if I am willing to receive Compassion, I must be courageous enough to let it flow through me to others.

Lord, grant me the grace of Compassion, and the Courage to act on the authority of that grace. I know this is not a silent grace. It is a grace of action, and it will not allow me to be still when facing human suffering. But if I hope to be treated with Compassion by others, I must open my heart to serve others in kind. I cannot live in fear of the power of this grace.

3

PRAY *and* IT SHALL *be* GIVEN

Prayer

I SPENT THIS DAY IN DEEP reflection about the intimacy of the Divine in my life, about necessary personal counsel. In the prayer, I released my hands from the steering wheel of my life, requesting that the Divine take over. I could feel that I was being directed to do something, to see something clearly—but what was it? Finally I uttered the powerful prayer "Take charge. I cannot see my way." Whatever needed to be released from my life, whatever needed to happen, I would not look back. I would only go forward. Within hours, a seemingly small incident occurred. Then it escalated. By morning, a heart-shattering event resulted. The answer had arrived. My life was drastically changed—just like that. I had been going on one path, planning for one future, and now I was on a different path, planning for a different future. Just like that. I retreated by habit, by spiritual gravity, into the silence of my interior castle. I was breathless from heaven's response, its speed and holy intimacy. I was confused—why allow me to go in that other direction in the first place? Now a part of my life just evaporated. I had asked for clarity. I had asked heaven to take charge. Now I must gather the pieces of the consequences. In my inner castle, I sensed the fracturing of my heart. And then—just like that—heaven sent in the remedy. The comforting presence of beloved friends poured in. I let that love flood into my heart, like a salve on an open wound. I felt myself fall even deeper into mystical silence. I was now just a witness to the two sides of my heart—one fractured, one absorbing love. I remember the myth of the two wolves in a dark, cold cave, one pacing with bitterness and the other calmed by love. The cave dweller must select one to represent the consequence of the injury life had just given him. Which one will carry the wound out of the cave—the wolf of bitterness or the wolf of love? In times past, I have chosen bitterness. I've watched that wolf leave the cave on my behalf. I wanted the wolf to attack the world as it had wounded me. I would not be responsible for those attacks—for who can control a wolf? But it did not turn out as I imagined. The wolf only bit *me*, again and again. Wiser today, I chose the wolf that carried love. I visualized a silk thread mending my heart in the darkness of the cave, careful not to seal it completely closed. I mended it just enough to stop the bleeding. I dwelled in awe and gratitude that one prayer, uttered in silence while standing in my kitchen, had been heard with such speed. Whispers reach heaven. I stayed in the silence of my cave for a long time, healing the fractured side of my heart. And then I felt my rich creature nature rise up and take its place once again in the vast expanse of me, turning this inner cave into my brilliant interior castle. I felt its sparkle and life force ripple into every cell of my being, animating every perception. I could feel my essential self rising from the debris of the life I thought I was going to have, which was already fading from view. I could feel the whole of myself fully: *This is who I am in this lifetime. Know thyself and you will know the Universe.* I bow to You, Lord. To Your intimate presence in my life.

Guidance

We often wonder how it is that prayers are answered; how long it will take for prayers to be answered; and whether our prayers will be answered at all. We seek signs and look for proof, usually for indications that the Earth has moved in the ways we wanted it to move. When nothing seems to change in front of our eyes—or worse, when unplanned events occur—we either question the wisdom of heaven or tell ourselves that praying is of no use. Regardless, prayers are answered immediately. That we do not see how is of no importance to heaven. Events may unfold that in the moment strike us as catastrophic. Heaven plays the long game. And—though this is difficult to comprehend—our happiness is not a divine priority. While it is of the greatest interest to us, the value system of the divine realm is focused on bringing us into a state of conscious balance, health, and awareness of the quality of our actions and choices. Happiness is the end product of those attributes of the soul.

Grace

It takes the grace of Trust to turn your life over to the forces of heaven. "Take charge. I cannot see my way." A simple prayer, the most powerful of all.

Grant me the grace of Trust, Lord, in You and in my own soul—for that is the vessel through which You speak to me. The truth is, I do trust that You answer my prayers. It is me I do not trust to listen and act on Your guidance.

4

KEEP *Me* HUMBLE

Prayer

KEEP ME HUMBLE, LORD. Keep me ever mindful that I am not the center of this Universe. I am not the sun, and these planets do not revolve around me. No one was born to serve me, and life does not owe me a thing. How can life owe anyone anything? And yet, this is a planet populated with human beings who believe that life owes them something special. Who or what, I wonder, is this force of life that is supposed to deliver the goods to them? You? How is it that we have come to believe we are owed something from life? I have witnessed the suffering of so many people who direct their precious life force toward collecting on a debt—and rarely do they emerge victorious. Pride is poison, and I have felt that poison flow through my veins all too often. I have experienced the fires that pride can ignite, all of them destructive. I have finally learned that it is far better to walk in gratitude for what I have than to dwell on what I think I *should* have or on what has been taken from me. And yet, even knowing that truth, pride can erupt so easily. But I have also learned that love silences pride. Reminding myself of what I love about someone, or about all that is good in my life, unlocks the grip of a momentary eruption of pride. I do not want to waste my energy on the illusions that pride can create in my thoughts. Life is just too brief a journey to rise in the morning and walk backward into the past. Keep me humble, Lord. There is great freedom in releasing the illusion that the world spins around me.

Guidance

It is not easy to walk humbly on the Earth. And yet the great spiritual paradox is that humbleness is our greatest protection, mostly from ourselves. So much of our suffering is brought about through acts of personal hubris, through the fear of being humiliated, and because we are unable to admit our own failings. The result is that we are driven to acts of trying to control what cannot be controlled: other people and the outcomes of events in life. We are never free as a result. We dwell in stress and anxiety and the fear of the loss of a control we never had in the first place. Humility is not poverty but the wealth of freedom that comes when we release judgment of others.

Grace

Humility is a grace, one we need more often than we realize. When you feel the fire of pride or arrogance erupting in you, ask for the grace of humbleness to pour into you and put out that fire. Close your eyes and tell yourself to "humble up"—and then re-engage in the world around you.

Lord, grant me the grace of Humility. Keep me ever mindful of what I am capable of when my hubris rises to the surface, and the harm I can do—to others and myself—when I imagine that I am powerless.

5

WHERE Are YOU, LORD?

Prayer

LORD, I WOKE UP with the images of lost children on my mind and in my heart. I find I cannot sleep very well these days. After hearing the news today about the mistreatment of children, I felt guilty sleeping in my own bed. I am enraged with guilt and anger and disbelief. I am too old to wonder where You are, Lord, or to ask, "How can You allow this to happen?" This is *our* doing. This is who we are. As I thought about that this morning, I worried I would break in despair. Then I heard the "ding" from my phone, indicating someone had sent me an e-mail message. Someone had sent me a brief talk given by a man who had a near-death experience. I rarely pay attention to such e-mail messages, especially from strangers. But I was feeling so sad, so helpless, that I lacked the energy to get out of my chair. So, I listened. I'll cut to the chase, Lord . . . I *believed* the message from this sweet, unassuming man who said he met Jesus in his near-death experience. He was allowed to ask one question of Jesus. He asked, "So, what's the purpose of life?" Jesus told him that love was the only true reason to have life: to experience the power of love. Something about that message felt as if it had been delivered directly to my heart, Lord. What I am overwhelmed with is the absence of love. This, too, is a measure of the power of love—the despair we feel when we are living in its absence. Grant me the capacity to generate love in my life. Not just when I am loved, or when I'm with the people I love, but for the *sake* of love—for love's power to defeat the worst instincts in human nature.

Guidance

Love is the most difficult of all life's lessons, probably because it is the only true lesson we have to learn. Either we use love in our choices—or we do not. Either we think with love, or we don't. Either we speak with love, or we speak the opposite. Everything else is the consequence of those choices. Even in the midst of viewing horror, it is important to pray for the courage and capacity to respond with love in some way. Waiting for life—or other people—to be perfect in order to open your heart is not the way of love. Imagine someone else deciding not to be loving toward you because of your clothing, your looks, or your way of life. Then look upon a stranger with a new and open heart.

Grace

Acting with love requires great Courage. The grace of Courage can feel as if it is exploding through our hearts at times, eclipsing our reason and motivating us to act in ways our rational mind could never imagine. But that is the nature of grace—an unimaginable force that moves us to act in larger-than-life ways that serve others, often more than ourselves.

God, grant me the grace of Courage to act in and with love.
I don't always associate courage with love. But the truth is, it takes
great courage to be a loving person for no reason other than
because love is the highest calling of a human being.

6

LORD, HOW CAN *this* HAPPEN?

Prayer

LORD, JUST WHEN I THINK I am filled with faith—and all things are as they should be in my life—something unexpected happens. Within seconds, doubt erupts inside me. Suddenly I am asking You, "How can this happen?" And I fully expect an answer. What exactly do I expect to hear from You? Time and again I have reflected upon other moments—or days—in my life when doubt has taken hold of the wheel of my reality like some bold teenager. I review how I cycled through panic and spent sleepless nights praying for an explanation. I wonder how many times I have asked You, "How can this happen?" I can truthfully say that You have never once given me a direct response. But You *have* responded; I can also truthfully say that. Your silence forces me to wait . . . to observe . . . to come to the realization each time that I am not in charge of all the countless events that make up the journey of my life, much less the lives of others. I am not in charge of anything. Your silence has allowed me to observe changes unfolding in the lives of others, not just mine. How can these and other events happen? Because they must. Change clears debris. Change moves us forward. Change is the nature of life. Lord, I know I am going to panic again—and again after that. And I will ask that question of You again. When I do, please remind me that each time this happened in the past, life moved on. Rebirth happened and joy always returned.

Guidance

Change is constant. Observe how much of your creative energy you direct into trying to control the changes unfolding in your life or into preventing things from happening. The wise choice is to prepare yourself from within to be able to handle any change that comes your way. We cannot control the external world, ours or anyone else's. We can only examine our inner responses again and again. The Buddha teaches that attachment to the world is a source of great suffering. That is an eternal truth. Every day we arise into a new world and we start our life again.

Grace

Wonder is an enchanting grace. Wonder lifts our spirits into the realm of our imagination. For a moment we experience the perfection of life. We drench ourselves in the possibility of what life could be like . . . *if only*. If only the power of the human spirit were unleashed to create—without doubt, and free of fear and greed. We are given the grace of Wonder because, as it turns out, everything we wonder about *is* possible. For the soul that partners with the power of heaven, anything is possible.

Lord, grant me the grace of Wonder. Rather than fearing change and the unknown, let me embrace the unknown with a sense of Wonder. Instead of closing down and fearing the worst, let the grace of Wonder open my imagination and my senses. Life runs on cycles. All things come to an end, and yet, every end means a new beginning. Beginnings are filled with opportunities to make different choices, to reboot, to start anew. Lord, let the grace of Wonder flow abundantly in my psyche and soul, especially during the times when I feel most vulnerable.

7

MOURNING *the* LOSS *of* FAMILY

Prayer

TODAY, LORD, A MEMBER OF MY FAMILY left us and came home to You. We shall grieve her passing for a long time. I knew she was dying. At times, I could see she *wanted* to die. Not because her physical pain was so great, Lord, but because her soul wanted to leave. She knew it, and she was forcing her soul to stay here a while longer. We could not let each other go. I am so sad. And yet, I am deeply aware that she could feel Your light calling her home. She mentioned it to me. And once, just once, she saw Your light and said, "Not yet, please." Maybe You let her stay a few more weeks? Or maybe You wanted her to get a glimpse of where she was going. I do know that she was not afraid at all. She had a calmness about her, a knowingness that You would be waiting for her. I am picturing her with You now. Like all of us who come into life and then return home again, I imagine an endless flow of souls to and from this Earth. Her passing reminds me yet again of how brief—and precious—each life is. It is difficult for me to comprehend that her life has come to an end, but that is how quickly life is over. Just like that. We mourn, Lord, because we cannot comprehend the swiftness of our own lifetime. Lord, keep me mindful that being alive is a gift—a precious gift—and that no day of my life will ever come again.

Guidance

With every passing of a loved one, we learn again the value of love, of kindness, of compassion. We take nothing with us, absolutely nothing. No amount of acquired goods can extend our lives one extra day. We recall love in the last stages of life, and it is love that carries us through the months of mourning. Do not invest one ounce of your energy in being prideful or angry. Those dark energies create deep regrets. Waste no time on them. Be a loving person.

Grace

The grace of Endurance energizes our coping abilities. Sometimes willpower alone is not enough. We require holy, divine resources. Then we can endure unthinkable challenges and inner sufferings. No prayer makes the challenges we must endure go away. No prayer instantly makes all things in our life fair or just. Life is too big a theater. *Karma* has an eternity of reasons for why things happen as they do. It is for us to endure the single moment or day or even lifetime we are passing through.

Grant me the grace of Endurance, Lord. Let this grace be with me in each breath I take, even as I walk through difficult moments. Remind me that nothing lasts forever, not even the most difficult passages of life.

8

THE CHOICE *to* NOT BE NEGATIVE, *for* JUST ONE DAY

Prayer

LORD, IT IS SO EASY TO BE disappointed in people and in the outcomes of projects. It is effortless to be a critical person. Why is that? Why is it so easy to be a negative person? People often tell me they need a reason to be positive. How can they feel good without a reason? Feeling good doesn't happen by itself. But somehow, Lord, I notice that we can feel negative without a reason. Just like that, we can sink into sadness or despair. We have become attached to the illusion that feeling positive requires something to first be perfect. We require a perfect day or a perfect outcome, or we must look perfect. Imperfection keeps positive sensations from rising out of one's heart. But perfection is impossible, Lord. And that's a wise truth. That means everything in life is *equally imperfect*. That, in itself, is a perfect truth. Today I am making the choice to not be negative about anything or anyone. Today I will see my world through the lens that *all is as it should be*. I will rise to the higher mystical truth: Events unfold impersonally. Events are not designed around a single person's karma or life purpose. I will remind myself of this truth today, every time I slip into "all about me" thinking. If a person gets angry with me today, I will remind myself that her anger has a history that does not involve me, just as my dark emotions have a history that is rarely connected to the people I encounter each day. If I stay in the present moment, free of yesterday's sadness or angry feelings, I will stay positive. Every new moment is pure, fresh energy. Lord, help me enter into the powerful experience of living in the moment. Of being fully present in the consciousness of my own life. That is the path to dwelling in positive energy because present-ness is only positive.

It is pure *prana*. Hover over me, Lord, through this day. Keep me ever mindful that one positive choice has the power to heal the life of a human being.

Guidance

Consider today an experiment in observing your own behaviors and habits. We rarely observe the speed of our reactions to others, or how rapidly a negative attitude takes possession of our mind. We learn about ourselves by watching ourselves as if we were outsiders. Ask yourself, *Why did I say that? What is my real agenda with that person? Why did I make a negative comment? Why am I judging this situation?* Ultimately, all these questions have the same answer: We are fearful of how something different can change the order of our life. We prefer to let our insecurities direct us, rather than the truth. Observe this in yourself today.

Grace

It takes an enormous amount of the grace of Determination to examine your own actions, thoughts, and beliefs. Such interior quests are what Teresa of Ávila called "the search for self-knowledge." That, for her, was the way of perfection, the path to your interior castle, your soul. Pursuing your own inner truth is the only true quest in life. Your life changes when you decide to pursue who you are and what it is God wants of you. Everything else is a *who-done-it* or a *what-else-is-there* or a *why-did-this-happen-to-me?*

---

*Lord, grant me the Determination to stay positive,
even for this day. I would not think that feeling good about life
would be such an effort. But I realize, more and more, that it is a
choice. And it takes a great deal of Determination to not slip into
negative thinking or self-pity or some other dark thought-pit. It is so
easy to give way to darkness. We just have to give up.*

9

EMBRACING *Inner* SILENCE

Prayer

LORD, I DEVOTE THIS DAY to inner silence. Even silence is guidance. It has taken me years to appreciate the messages hidden in silence. I am now making the choice to be a person who does not require constant instructions, constant feedback, constant reinforcement from You or from friends and family. I used to hope and wait for that type of guidance, as if You were an off-planet parent. There was a time when I *wanted* You to be an off-planet parent, a powerful force that protected me from my own foolish decisions. Now I know that nothing could be more preposterous than to imagine You looking like, or behaving as, a huge invisible human being. I have only the slightest idea of what You are. You are an eternal mystery, an impersonal Light with countless manifestations. And yet somehow, I also know You are lovingly aware of all that You have created. All creation matters to You. I know that truth from my observations of the perfection of nature. Some perfect cosmic authority organized the system of life. That had to be You. Cruelty is not woven into the perfection of nature. Cruelty is a flaw, a defect. We are free to blend into the perfection of Your holy design, to move with the cycles of life, to allow death and rebirth, sunrises and sunsets to happen again and again as You ordered these cycles, or we can choose to break away from the patterns of life and suffer. I can dwell in the comfort of that truth for the rest of my life. That is not a silent thought or a quiet truth, Lord. That truth is pure celestial music . . . all creation matters. All creation is holy, sacred, meaningful. All creation is subject to the order of Nature, to the order of You. Your nature is hidden in Nature itself. I enter that thought as if it were a secret portal. Life becomes animated. I imagine every creature smiling back at me.

As if they can see—by the look of awe on my face—that I have found the God-thread holding this Universe together. That God-thread runs through all of us like a daisy chain. Lord, how you must be amused by the way we human beings do our calculations about life! Today I will dwell in celestial silence, knowing that I am in the company of angels and saints—and You.

Guidance

We are subject to the laws of nature. The laws of balance, cause and effect, and opposites work their authority into all of our choices. The handiwork of co-creation is present in our every breath, in every action we initiate. We cannot act separately from the whole of life. So rest in silence and observe your sense of inner balance. Note when and how you lose that balance, what choices serve to maintain it, and what actions and thoughts compromise it. Inner balance is the core magnet to the flow of your life force.

Grace

Surrender is one of the great graces of the Divine. We do not give up when we surrender. Not at all. Surrender is an act of recognition, an acknowledgement of the order of the Universe. We surrender our power to God as the act of ultimate trust, consciously merging the power of our soul with the order of the Universe. We consciously step into the flow of our lives and into the conscious stream of guidance and grace that is already flowing through our soul. Surrender is an act of awakening.

Lord, grant me the ability to understand the true meaning of the grace of Surrender, so that I may one day utter the prayer "I surrender unto You all that I am"—and truly mean it.

10

I BREATHE *with* ALL *Living* CREATURES

Prayer

LORD, TODAY MY PRAYER IS "I breathe with all living creatures." I will dwell in the mystical truth that I share the breath of creation with all sentient beings. I am beginning to comprehend the rules of co-creation. Little by little, I observe that each choice I make sets either divine light—or darkness—into motion. I am not alone in this Universe, even though I sometimes feel that I am. My thoughts and emotions belong to everyone. Somehow, in some way, the energy of all beings passes through me like wind through a field of flowers. We all share this Earth and participate in the creation of every event. Nothing could be more preposterous than to believe any of us is separate, safe, or immune from acts of creation or destruction. What is in one is in the whole. I wonder, Lord, why we are repelled by that sacred truth. Why do we not want to be one with all beings? If I could see clearly, Lord, I would see that my energy is everywhere. I have left millions of tiny particles of my energy, like cosmic crumbs, in every country, city, town, and home I have visited, not to mention every street I have ever walked upon. The same is true for everyone else. We are always blending together—a great cosmic weave of living power. No wonder the great mystics finally surrendered to You, Lord. They wanted You to take charge of this immense power of creation that is set into motion with every breath we take. Today, Lord, I will breathe with all creation. I will dwell in the truth that I am one with all life. And all life is one with me.

Guidance

The great spiritual masters emphasized the mystical truth that all is one. That truth cannot be grasped intellectually. Mystical truths are experienced. We are invited into the power of a mystical truth. That is called a mystical experience. Teresa of Ávila often seemed as if she had become a corpse when she had a mystical experience. Upon returning to consciousness, her community of nuns would ask, "Mother, where did you go?" but she could not describe what her soul had experienced. Trying to explain to her sisters why she could not elaborate, she once responded, "I wanted to take my brain (mind) with, but it just could not make the journey." We cannot comprehend the mystical truth of being interconnected with all sentient beings. We can only make the choice to live as if it were the truth and observe whether somehow that choice gradually influences the quality of our life for the better.

Grace

Compassion is a grace that allows for the flow of impersonal love toward others. Compassion expands your heart and anesthetizes your judgment of others. You are often inspired with the desire to embrace the other, but not from sentiment or pity. Rather, the deeper humanitarian cords that unite us as human beings animate within you.

Lord, Compassion is a powerful grace. It does not discriminate. Having a compassionate heart can be risky. But what other choice is there? If I look upon others with harsh judgment, I must imagine myself in their shoes—because what I do to another person, I am doing to myself. So, open my heart to Compassion, Lord. Hover over me with endless guidance as I learn to live as one with all sentient beings.

11

Make ME RESILIENT

Prayer

I MARVEL AT THE RESILIENCE of nature, Lord. No matter where I look, I see a theater of life in motion. I wonder what my life looks like from a distance. What would I see if I could view my life through a wide, cosmic lens? Would I even comprehend the significance of all the many currents of life flowing to me? Those avoiding me as well as those that would appear to embrace me? I suspect I would observe that the flow of life—the continuum of life—does not stop for anything or anyone. No one's problems or heartaches or resentments are important enough or unique enough to stop or shift the natural rhythms and cycles of life. Forests burn and then produce new growth. Earthquakes shape the Earth anew. Land rises and falls. No natural form of life mourns the organic shifting of the sands of time except us humans, Lord. Again and again, Lord, we plant our feet firmly on shaking ground, determined to stop fires in the forest and erupting earthquakes from their task of breaking new ground wide open. Because we do not want our lives, our personal worlds, to change.

I sometimes want to stop the cycles of life myself, Lord. I am not sure when those cycles will collapse the walls of my own life or bring some part of it to a complete halt. I am not certain I have the resilience to start anew, again and again, as nature does. And yet, I have experienced the grace of Resilience flooding into my blood and bones in the exact second when I need it most. Just when I felt despair approach the energy of my heart, suddenly—in an instant—all I could think was, *Everything will be fine.* Despair shattered like fragile glass. I wondered how I had come up with such a positive thought—much less that I actually *believed* it. Somehow in that moment, I not only believed that all would be well—I knew it. With all my heart and soul. For me, the crisis that had so frightened me ended in that instant. I felt Your message melt into me: *I will be fine. Everything will be fine.* I knew I had to relinquish my idea about wanting a certain outcome and let the wisdom plan of my life take over. Whatever I had to deal with as far as people and the everyday details of life felt like ordinary paperwork. It is exhausting to try to control all the rivers that flow into my life. The better choice is to become a good passenger, skilled in navigating the cycles of nature. For as we become one with all nature, we find our way to You.

Guidance

Each day we have endless opportunities to apply the grace of Resilience. It takes Resilience to decide to initiate a new pattern in your life because you must battle the part of you that will not let go of the old pattern. It takes Resilience to continue to nurture a creative vision that only you believe in. It takes the grace of Resilience to get up in the morning when you are overwhelmed with problems. The organic design of living creatures is to be resilient: to survive, adjust, and find a way through difficulties. We can't accept defeat because we each have a phoenix in us that calls us to rise again and again from the ashes of challenge and despair. We are born to be resilient.

Grace

Resilience is a powerful grace that enhances our natural instincts to get up and try again. It offers us a "blink of an eye" chance to reimagine our thinking, or our attitude, through a positive lens. This grace is like a booster shot we receive when our psychic immune system is depleted. As a result we can feel suddenly hopeful and re-energized, and can even experience a diminishing of physical aches and pains.

*Lord, I have felt the grace of Resilience pour into me
during some of my weakest moments. I know this grace.
And that is why I am asking for the grace of Resilience to come
into my soul at this time in my life. I need to feel the hand of heaven
helping me rise again, lifting me from the depths of my sense that
everything is overwhelming. For heaven, nothing is overwhelming.
I need that truth to be set on fire within me again.*

12

CONFRONTING MY *Frightened* INNER SELF

Prayer

TODAY I REMINDED MYSELF of the brilliant teachings of Teresa of Ávila, as I do on most days. But something today brought to mind her description of the interior of the third mansion of our soul. She said that the insidious reptile of our own stubborn nature dwells right there in the middle of our body. That gut-dwelling reptile will fight to keep us in our smallest attitude—reducing us to superstitious ways of thinking—so we remain fearful of making outrageous, courageous decisions. Lord, these reptiles prevent us from acting on our inner guidance, even though we can perceive that guidance. We can always sense Your guidance, especially through our gut. No wonder that the gut is the favorite dwelling place for our reptiles. Teresa said reptiles see better at night than we do, so we need to get them into the light. We need to draw out our reptiles, to disarm them.

So, my prayer for today, Lord, is to breathe out the reptile of my frightened self, that part of me that sees the world in small and limited ways. Fear makes me think and act in ways that diminish the quality of my life. Most of my fears, Lord, have never come to pass. These fears are truly reptiles: imaginary inner creatures that invade my thoughts like shadow figures, especially when I feel most vulnerable. But rarely have I experienced any of my fears rupturing into my life, Lord. I need to dwell in that truth, and let its power dissolve my inner reptiles.

Guidance

Teresa of Ávila said that once a reptile—a fear—gets into your mind, it takes great effort to get it to leave. All of us have had experiences with reptile invasion. Once a fear takes hold of our thinking, that fear can disguise itself as ordinary conversation, even presenting as a sound and logical way of thinking. Reptiles are clever. Prayer is a way of protecting yourself from reptile invasions; that is, prayer creates a field of grace around you. Like a subtle homeopathic moat around a castle, the protective influence of a field of grace allows you to recognize fear in another person for what it is. That single act of recognition is powerful enough to generate in you a type of detachment from that individual. It's as if you drew up the drawbridge to your castle, not allowing the fears of friends and strangers to enter your energy field. That sense of detachment, incidentally, need not be conscious. In fact, it usually isn't.

Grace

The grace of Trust is one of the core graces of the soul. This grace has a way of focusing your attention on positive inner messages and reminders of the many ways you have always survived difficult situations. You might suddenly recall a time when you trusted your gut instincts and acted on them. Sometimes one reminder of a powerful choice you made based on trust is enough to silence your reptiles.

Lord, I have never been good at trusting others in my life.
Then I realized that my lack of trust was because I did not trust my
own instincts. And those inner instincts were ultimately my threads to
You, to Your voice guiding me. I need that thread to You, Lord, because
without that thread of Trust, I am driving my life without a compass.
I need to weave that thread to You, one choice at a time. So, grant me
the grace of Trust, Lord, to act on that small inner voice that guides
me ever so softly, even in the loudest times of chaos.

13

FINDING *Yet Another* TRUTH

Prayer

LORD, I LEARNED A WHILE ago that an encounter with even the smallest truth—although really there is no such thing as a small truth—changes the whole of my life. I remind myself daily of the power of truth. I believe we are "blinded by the truth" because truth is so potent. It did frighten me once to think about how fragile my life is. But now that same truth inspires me. It fills me with the desire to love the people in my life more and to be less judgmental about all the many insignificant challenges in life. Lord, grant me the courage to embrace truth in all ways. I have experienced the pain of watching my life instantly change when the power of a truth evaporated an illusion. Yet I have never once regretted letting go of that illusion. I need clarity to rise from my inner nature, my deeper self. I need to rely upon my inner guidance, Lord, most especially when I sense an illusion evaporating a part of my life that I thought was so real a second ago. What other source do I have for truth in this life but You?

Guidance

If we could see clearly, we would recognize that every moment in life contains an opportunity to see or understand something more clearly than we did before. When a day seems to be filled with difficult encounters, stop for a moment and observe what is really taking place right in front of you. Illusions are breaking down, and you cannot stop that process from happening. My counsel to people who are going through especially rough patches is to not fight the challenges but go along with everything they cannot stop. Nothing is personal about the movement of truth in our lives, though events do feel personal. But think of how often you get caught up in the events of another person's life before you realize it. We are as much participants in all that happens to others as so many others are participants in the events in our lives. And yet every event and conversation, and even the most intense emotion is with us for but a second. It is soon replaced by the next moment's content, and then the next. Not even pain stands still.

Grace

Gratitude is a lovely grace. It is more than thankfulness. The grace of Gratitude lifts a person into the realization that love, for example, is provided for us. We meet people who find something in us to love. We cannot make someone love us, and yet they do. There is no such thing as a casual encounter in which love emerges. Teresa of Ávila reminded her Sisters that everything—even love—was provided by God as a blessing. When difficulties come, as they always do, it is the grace of Gratitude that we should dwell in. Always head toward the light when you feel fear and darkness near you.

Lord, I should not need to ask for Gratitude. I should be bursting with this grace, knowing that even one person loves me— not to mention so many more. Sometimes I feel a downpour of Gratitude flush through me like vibrational rain. When I do, I always pause and wonder whether it's You reminding me that even the smallest details of my life are somehow known to You. Or perhaps that dwelling in this grace should be my natural resting place.

14

A TIME *for* HOLY LISTENING

Prayer

LORD, TODAY I WILL SPEND time in holy listening and silence. Today, I listen for the sound of how You express Yourself in my life. In ancient days You spoke through the wind, through fire, through storms and the movement of the Sun. The ancients saw You everywhere and in everything. They recognized Your presence in nature, in the forests and in the whisper of leaves rustling to sudden breezes. Our thinking today is that they were foolish, frightened human beings, little more than cave dwellers wandering a primitive Earth. But perhaps not. Perhaps they were really filled with clarity, unencumbered by doubt. They stood on a silent Earth, a clean, pure Earth, empty of noise. Everything was fresh and unpolluted. They saw You everywhere because You were everything to them. They recognized their vulnerability and were filled with the humbleness that came with dependence upon sacred power. I do not know how to listen for You in nature. I have grown accustomed to trusting my mind for instructions. I do not know how to find You in the many distractions and noise in my mind. I do not know how to be silent from within. But I will begin by creating a silent world around me. With closed eyes, I imagine myself approaching a holy well deep within me. I drop a single pebble into that well and listen for the delicate sound of one pebble slipping into the softness of the holy center of my being. There, in this sacred, silent, inner place, I shall wait for You.

Guidance

Inner silence is not the same as being quiet. Being quiet means that you are not speaking, or that you have removed yourself from external noise, or that you want to get away from chaos to be alone. Entering silence, on the other hand, is the choice to turn your attention inward with the intent to listen for the rustling of holy wind in your soul. Holy listening is listening "below" your head. Release the endless questioning nature of your mind and breathe your attention into your solar plexus. You will have to do this again and again during the day because out of habit, you will kick into mental gear in a microsecond. If you are engaging in ordinary life activities today, you have to adapt sacred silence and holy listening to your world. It is never impossible to enter inner silence or to retreat to your holy center. In fact, what could be more important than to realize you can retreat to your holy center while conducting business or shopping, or during a stressful exchange with someone? You do not have to flee to a remote place to recharge and protect yourself. Your soul is resourceful; it is a vessel for guidance and grace. Should you find yourself in such a circumstance today, close your eyes and repeat the prayer, "In this sacred inner space, I shall wait for You. I am waiting, Lord. I am listening."

Grace

Holy Silence is a grace. It is the grace that stops us from saying words that we cannot take back, that cause irreparable damage. Holy Silence is a grace that can descend upon us in the midst of great confusion, drawing us immediately inward to stillness, often just long enough to gather our emotions and thoughts. If you have ever been grateful for having *not* said something—because you heard a voice inside you asking, "Are you sure you want to say that?"—then you have experienced this powerful grace.

Lord, I will wait for You in the bliss of holy Silence.
Drenched in this grace, I will rest in inner quietude—not waiting
for answers or signs or signals. I will know You by tranquility.

15

BLESS *this* JOURNEY
THAT IS MY LIFE

Prayer

LORD, BLESS MY JOURNEY today as I go deeper into the vast territory of my soul. Just when I think I know myself, I discover a stranger living inside me. I must accept the truth that I am an endless, unknown creature, even to myself—perhaps *especially* to myself. With every new experience, I have to wonder, *How will I cope? How will I respond to that? What will I say?* I can never be certain what I will do next. There is so much about myself that I do not yet know or understand. Why, then, should chaos surprise me? I am spinning in a wind tunnel, watching the fragments of my life rush by. It is not up to You to stop these fragments. There is no prayer that will move heaven to piece together the odds and ends of my life. But You have given me that authority. It is up to me to become more aware, more attentive, more focused. That is my decision. Clarity of mind and soul will change how I live my life. A chaotic life ends up tossed about by fate. But clear-mindedness leaves room for courage and bold choices. Self-knowledge is the pathway to the soul. So, take me down deep, Lord, and reveal to me my true self.

Guidance

One of the more incomprehensible truths in life is that we are strangers to ourselves. We are not born knowing ourselves. We discover who we are through our own life experiences and relationships. We are never finished getting to know ourselves. That is perhaps the core truth that makes commitments so risky: nothing about us is certain or permanent. The wise person pursues the truth about his or her nature and cooperates with the governing laws of life. The Buddha taught, for instance, that change is constant and that attempting to stop something from changing, dying, or progressing is the source of suffering. The wise person embraces the governing laws of life and uses them as a guide. While living in harmony with nature cannot prevent pain or loss from happening in your life, that wise lifestyle choice can greatly reduce the unnecessary suffering that comes from working against the laws of nature.

Grace

Wisdom is a renowned grace, one of the first graces noted again and again in the Old Testament. Wisdom is the grace that brings a human being into contact with the collective experience of all humanity, into an encounter with the Akashic records. We have all met "wise souls." The grace of Wisdom comes through their eyes or their words; they are often far too young for words so profound. Great people are remembered for their Wisdom. One wise teaching has the power to inspire people for generations. "He who does not learn from the past is destined to repeat it." That wise truth is as applicable for the journey of a single life as it is for the journey of a nation. Wisdom is among the most essential graces of the human experience.

Lord, grant me the grace of Wisdom. Open the eyes of my soul to the jewels of truth and knowledge that I have gained in the experiences of my life so I may take my hard-earned wisdom with me all the days of my life.

16

FINDING TRUTH *in* ALL WAYS

Prayer

LORD, FINDING THE TRUTH in all ways—especially in myself and in my life—is the most rigorous task of all. An encounter with even the smallest truth changes the whole of my life. It always has, and it always will. I used to believe some things would go on forever, but the truth is, nothing is forever except the cycles of life and death—which are a manifestation of You. You show Yourself in every expression of life. You speak constantly through the cycles of life, as if they were organic covenants with us. You promise us a spring after every winter, hope after every difficulty, a rebirth after we crumble into ashes. I used to believe that life was a long journey. But the truth is that it is a day-by-day—and sometimes minute-by-minute—experience of breathing, interpreting my world, and deciding in that moment whether I am going to be afraid or not. My world looks beautiful when I feel safe and terrifying when I do not. Oddly, regardless of how I feel, the same trees are in view from my window. Clouds still pass overhead. Flowers are still blooming in my garden. The only variable is whether I wake in anxiety or in trust. It is day to day, this business of being alive. It is an illusion to believe I will be here tomorrow, even though I plan for it. Which will unfold? I can only wake tomorrow—or not. And yet knowing that truth makes me want to live more fully and more deeply each day. Instead of giving in to a fearful thought form, I am learning that most of my fears never come to pass. So I let the thought forms pass through me, like reading a bad menu at a restaurant I refuse to enter. It did frighten me once to think about how fragile life is. But now I prefer to draw inspiration from that truth, to dwell in gratitude for everyone and everything in my life. That is my power over fear-filled thought forms. I choose to dwell in grace, in appreciation of the truth that fear is a thought form but the holy power within me is real.

Guidance

Life is a very brief journey. Very brief. We can either be intimidated by that truth or we can be inspired to live life to the fullest. A jewel of truth is hidden in every moment in life. We can pause and ask, "What is really going on here?" or "What is the deeper reason why I am responding as I am?" There is no end to the quest for truth in our lives or, as the Buddha would say, the breakdown of our illusions. It is a long road to becoming an empty vessel. This journey requires endless endurance, for there is nothing simple about encounters with truth.

Grace

Endurance is a grace we need for many reasons. While we may associate Endurance with getting through life's many inescapable trials, it also helps us pursue a more authentic understanding of who we are, what motivates us, and why we believe what we do. Self-examination is the backbone of the spiritual journey: an endless quest to truly realize—and in turn, consciously take charge of—the power of our own soul. And this inner journey is indeed one that requires Endurance, as the task of continual examination of our motivations, our choices, and the quality of our thoughts never ends.

Lord, grant me the grace of Endurance: the ability to endure discovering the whole of who I am. Little by little, I observe that even the tone of my voice has consequences in the life of another human being. I can no longer tell myself that I am powerless if even the tone of voice I use makes a difference in another person's life. I need the grace of Endurance to even absorb that truth, as it requires so much of me. I must walk softly among all creatures, enduring negative actions without responding in kind. No wonder the great masters warned their disciples that this journey of awakening was one of agony and ecstasy, and that it could only be endured with constant prayer and infusions of grace.

17

GIVE UP *the* NEED *to* KNOW WHY

Prayer

LORD, THE OTHER DAY I saw the aftermath of a car accident. I had to drive slowly around two smashed vehicles surrounded by police cars. I moved by the scene at walking speed even though I was driving. I said a prayer for the injured people and then I wondered, *Why did this happen to them?* The next day I heard some local neighborhood news about a teenager committing suicide and I wondered again, *Why, Lord, did that young boy take his life? Why wasn't some angel sent in to help him?* And, of course, I have a list of "why" questions for You, Lord, that I ask all the time. But I realized something today. Each time I ask You, *Why?* I must make up an answer of my own. I have learned by now that You do not answer questions; You answer prayers. So, today I will release the need to know why things happen as they do, Lord. Releasing that one question frees me from many of the mysteries of the past I still hold on to, hoping that one day I will know why certain things happened in my life. Giving up the need to know why allows me to be present to all the many wonders that are unfolding in my life in *this* moment. Lord, it takes great trust and a surplus of patience to not ask why. And yet, I am realizing more and more that there is such freedom in releasing that part of me that endlessly searches for answers that will never be given. Lord, hover over me with grace and guidance as I devote this day to empowering my soul.

Guidance

At a deep level, we seek to know why things happen as they do because then we can strategize ways to prevent the unknowable—and the unstoppable—from happening to us. Since the earliest recorded times, human beings have wondered about the nature of the sacred realm. Are the gods like us? Do they act like us, think like us, mate like us? Absent any evidence, we projected our life-style onto the gods—but times a hundred. If we are loving, fair, and just, then the gods must be *very* loving, *extremely* fair, and *always* just. The gods are us on cosmic steroids. So it only makes sense that we would expect explanations from the heavens for events that shock, surprise, or traumatize us. We believe that if we are good, bad things should not happen to us. That is our law, after all. But when the events of our life fall out of harmony with the natural order of cause and effect, action and reaction, and choice and consequence—so far as we can see, at least—it is only logical that we turn our eyes upward toward the cosmos and demand to know, *Why?* After all, we created a logical, fair, and just God in our image and likeness. We feel entitled to explanations. But perhaps it is our understanding of the nature of God that must be examined when such a crisis makes us wonder. Perhaps divine wisdom and logic follow laws that span lifetimes and not just the here and now. Every lifetime includes all lifetimes. Every choice we have made is hidden in every consequence. We are incapable of the calculations required to understand the mathematics of karma.

Grace

The grace of Trust gives us the capacity to defy even what our eyes and ears tell us. Trust springs from deep within our gut and flows to our heart. Trust is not an intellectual grace; it is a survival grace. It gives us the stamina to hold on through challenging times and to endure difficult experiences. Because in our gut and heart, we can sense and trust that there is purpose to what—and why—things happen as they do.

Lord, grant me the grace to give up wanting to know why things happen as they do. This requires the grace of Trust. I must Trust in the whole story and not just the page I am reading or living that day. You hold the book of my life in Your hands; I live it one day at a time. I must Trust that You, as the author, know far more than I.

18

MELITING *through* REASON

Prayer

LORD, THIS BUSINESS OF NEEDING a reason for why things happen as they do is getting old. I find great peace in not needing to ask that question as much these days. I know from experience that You do not answer questions like that. Most humans don't even answer questions like that. Things happen as they happen for all sorts of reasons. Nothing happens without cause, but how many causes are there for everything I see? A plant has how many ancestor seeds? And how many processes in nature have to occur before a leaf unfolds on a branch in springtime? I haven't a clue. I imagine that every activity, every thought, every voice that fills every moment of my life has taken countless acts of preparation to unfold in that moment as it did. And the slightest change any-where along those endless paths—which may go back lifetimes— could have shifted what took place in this moment right now. I know this Universe is as complex and wondrous as that. Which means, Lord, that this holy Universe is spontaneous, creative, interactive, and responsive. It is alive within me, and I with it. This entire Universe is Your living Being. I cannot comprehend that truth, but I can think about it. I can dwell in it, which I do when I pray with You like this. Even imagining such a thought is somehow wildly comforting. This is a mystically conscious, holy Universe, a wondrously ordered cosmic residence that is not ruled or regulated by the reasoning minds of humans. What could be more obvious? Asking for reasons for why one thing happened as it did would appear all the more absurd when I hang that request like a Post-it note against the background of creation. Lord, keep me from becoming a prisoner of my own mind. I prefer to dwell in my mystical imagination, where all things are possible with You.

No wonder the great mystics like Francis of Assisi and wondrous Teresa of Ávila fell so deeply in love with You and all creation. You *were* all creation to them.

Guidance

Nothing is more typically human than to seek instructions and guidance for the sake of personal safety. Why would we not project that need onto our idea of God? Even if we remind ourselves a hundred times that we have never received a direct answer for that prayer-request, still, in difficult or painful times we are inclined to cast our eyes toward the heavens and ask, "Why?" That is because all of us participate in a cosmic-sized illusion that unfair, unjust, or painful events should bypass us. Maybe we think we've already had our share of pain so we do not deserve more. Or maybe we think we've been so good all our lives that bad things should not happen to us at all. Whatever it is we tell ourselves, however, all that mindless chatter is just a personal narrative. Chatter never stops the wheel of life from turning as it will. The "why?" question can be answered, more often than not, by *us*. We need only have the courage to examine the field of choices and consequences in which we live and make decisions. Do we make wise or courageous choices? Do we live in ways that sabotage our own best interests? If we examined our suffering in microscopic detail, we would realize that much of it is our own handiwork. As difficult as it is to admit, a good amount of our suffering is self-inflicted. Consider the choices to nurture dark attitudes or unforgiving emotions, to make decisions based upon fear, or to live in denial that a cycle of our life has come to an end. Or we deny the truth about our shadow patterns, such as our addictions or our inability to tell the truth, or the consequences of acting on our wounded pride. Eventually these subtle but very powerful dark patterns weave themselves into a massive net that becomes that psychic atmosphere of our life. God is not the creator of that dark net; *we* are. Yet the extraordinary and even miraculous fact is that even the darkest web evaporates through the power of truth.

Grace

The grace of Courage has many expressions: action in battle, the Courage to speak out against evil, the Courage to try again and again. We also need Courage to confront patterns in ourselves that are self-defeating. Instead of asking heaven for reasons why things happen as they do in our lives, we must first have the Courage to examine the choices we have made along the way. Someone said to me, "And how was I supposed to choose to avoid a flood I did not see coming?" Fair enough. And yet I live in an area known for tornadoes and polar vortexes. I do not know when wild weather will erupt—but I do know it will. Wisdom tells me to be prepared for the climate I live in, as prepared as one can be within "reason," while also knowing that nature is more powerful than I am. We reside in two realms of reason, ours and God's. We must tend to our physical life reality and its many challenges. This includes examining with courage our reasons for why we do, speak, and act as we do—or do not. As for divine reasoning, that is a realm we will never enter, so stop knocking at that door.

Lord, grant me the Courage to break through my pattern of denial and self-deception, especially when it causes me to see my world in ways that are harmful to myself and others. I need the Courage to recognize that I am as likely as my neighbor to be hit by a storm. Nature doesn't play favorites, and that is a truth that takes Courage and Humility to accept.

19

FRACTURED *into* TRANQUILITY

Prayer

LORD, I BEGAN MY DAY emotionally fractured. I felt the pieces of myself scattered in my energy field like broken glass. I was distracted, unable to focus, in search of my center. Instinctively, I closed my eyes and took a deep breath—and turned inward. I needed to find my way back to my inner sanctuary, that well-worn path inside me that leads me away from distractions and into quietude. I remain awestruck by the power of a fracturing experience. For days and even weeks, I can feel the sensations of being present in my life, whole, not dwelling on anything from the past, not worried about events yet to come that I might never encounter anyway. And then suddenly, always unexpectedly, something happens, and I am reminded yet again that I have slipped into the illusion of thinking that I had accomplished a permanent state of sacred quietude, that I had somehow arrived at that inner peace that the cycles of change cannot reach. Blessed stillness flipped into swirling chaos the moment I learned of the health crisis of yet another family member. Questions I never thought I would have to deal with began presenting themselves to me for responses. Instantly, Lord, I am not my clear, conscious self—just when I need that part of myself the most. But I believe You are very much hidden—and very obvious—in all the events of my life, even when I am shattered by heartbreaking news. Perhaps some people think a coincidence is just a coincidence. Sometimes lines crossing in our lives might indeed be merely luck or a curious happening. But I have long considered luck a word that belongs to atheists and people who are afraid to look up and imagine You. I see You in those moments, especially when I am fractured—like I was the other night, wondering about the pros and cons of a medical protocol with which I was not familiar. In my fractured state, I could not concentrate enough to research information on it, much less remember anything I would read. I decided to turn on the news and discovered my television was on a channel I never watch. I wondered for a moment who had been tampering with my television, knowing that no one was in my home. And then I noticed what was on that channel. It was a talk show, and the host was interviewing a physician on the very treatment I was too exhausted to look into. I could not help but smile—and take notes. I felt the graces of hope and gratitude—and the sensation of awe—wash through me like a healing balm. I never want to cease being amazed by Your presence in my life, and I never am.

Guidance

The Buddha taught that our circumstances in life can shift in the blink of an eye. Just like that, the forces of life can shift us from rich to poor, from poor to rich, from married to single, from sad to happy, from imprisoned to free, from calm to chaos. Again and again life teaches us that we are not in charge of anything but our response to the many outside currents of life—all of which are impersonal, organic, and interconnected to the whole network of life. Yet somehow, within this endless, impersonal cosmic landscape of creation, how and when and why the events of your life unfold are intimately known to the Divine. They are purposeful. For nothing is random; nothing is without cause or consequence. Experiences commonly referred to as "synchronicity" —such as a television program broadcasting the exact information I desperately needed to understand—are, for me, mystical experiences. They are evidence of the intimacy with which we are watched and cared for by the Divine. Teresa of Ávila said, "Look for God in the small details of your life," in the ordinary world, in the most insignificant acts that make your life easier or safer or that provide that one detail that may well save the life of someone you love dearly. Through the mystical lens, anything might be a blessing in disguise.

Grace

The grace of Gratitude is ever soothing to your soul. Start small. Look for God in the smallest details of your life, shifting from the familiar Gratitude list of the big, known, and obvious. Carry a continual sense of Gratitude in you for fresh water, for a day without violence—if you are blessed enough to experience a day without violence—or for having enough food to eat and perhaps extra to share with someone who does not have as much. Live this grace. Express this grace in all your actions. It is never enough to just mentally say, *Thank you. Live* your Gratitude. And share this grace with others.

Lord, grant me the grace of Gratitude, especially when I fail to see all that is good in my life—most especially in those moments. I need to remind myself of all the many ordinary gifts in my life that are really not ordinary at all but true blessings. Even the ability to buy a cup of coffee when I want one is a blessing. All I have to do is turn on the television to witness people suffering, waiting upon the mercy of others for a meal or a drink. There but for the grace of God go I.

20

REFLECTIONS *on* EVIL

Prayer

LORD, WHAT DO I TELL PEOPLE who do not believe in evil? It is so easy for me to see the handiwork of evil and darkness in the world, the many clever ways in which it feeds the arrogance and blindness of human beings. I cannot help but notice how many of these people carry good luck charms or wear crystals for protection against what they perceive as "negativity" in their life. Used this way, *negativity* can be a smokescreen word. The word has no connection to the sacred. But to recognize an action or a personal agenda as evil—whose definition is *the conscious choice to do harm to another*—immediately puts one's soul on full alert. I have grown accustomed to my soul signaling me when I am in the presence of evil. I can feel when conscious, active darkness is trolling for an unsuspecting victim—or a willing companion. We so easily believe in goodness and in the presence of angels. I've seen the faces of people light up like children at the mention of having guardian angels hovering over them. Yet they cannot seem to comprehend that darkness has its own soldiers in the field, who equally utilize the laws of the universe. Darkness is attracted to darkness. Evil has many advantages in the physical world, Lord— or so it seems. An act of darkness tricks us, in that it satisfies a powerful urge: to have the power to control outcomes and other people, or to experience immediate gratification. But nothing that evil creates is supported by grace. Therefore, whatever is created by evil cannot endure for long. These truths are best taught through experience, as I have learned, Lord. It is wiser for me to *not* speak of evil, at least not directly. I recognize that even the word frightens people today—a reaction that sometimes indicates a person has had an experience with someone genuinely motivated by evil, or that this individual has *knowingly* compromised his or her own soul in some way. But I realized long ago that, just as Teresa of Ávila instructed her nuns to do, each day we must walk humbly on this Earth and ask for the grace of divine protection. For we cannot see or understand the mysteries of the invisible realm. And none of us truly knows the depth and power of our own shadow, especially when we are vulnerable. Therefore, we must ask for the grace of Protection to "lead us not into temptation" and to keep us ever mindful of our own weaknesses. Lord, I do not know the many occupants of the invisible realm, but I do know that the renowned spiritual masters prayed for protection and guidance. They were guides, all too familiar with the ways of darkness.

Guidance

Years ago I read a story in the newspaper about a man who extricated himself from a Satanic cult. He told the reporter that most people in Chicago would recognize the names of many of the people who were in that cult. The journalist wrote the article in a skeptical tone, not surprisingly. But in response to the reporter's skepticism, this former cult member commented, "Evil counts on people having your attitude, especially arrogance. That's exactly why demons are so powerful. You just don't believe they exist." I could feel the truth in that statement. All the time, our own arrogance or fear prevents us from believing or acknowledging truths about ourselves. We consider arrogance protection. The more we think we know, the more someone else must be wrong. It doesn't matter if we don't have the facts right—we just have to sound as if we know what we are talking about, and we have to keep talking. Anything to keep truth from our door. Because once truth gets in, the house of cards comes tumbling down. Evil does not manifest like a gargoyle hiding in the corner of a room at night. It enters into our consciousness through the same portals as inspiration: through our thoughts, our instincts, our conscience, and the workings of our inner nature. It comes in through the rotting energetic circuitry of self-pity narratives that get bigger and bigger, encouraging us to blame others for the despair in our lives. Or evil slips into our thoughts by telling us we are entitled to more and more, or that we don't deserve the misfortunes that have come our way, or that we have a right to hold others responsible for our unhappiness. The great skill of darkness is that it seeks to weaken us—our resolve, our stamina, our instincts, our character, and eventually our soul. The moment—the second—you sense yourself compromising who you are, recognize that sensation as a "soul alert." Check out how you feel when you say something that is not true or when you agree to something that actually does not sit well with you. Immediately you will recognize that you have gone on "soul alert"—a response that says *proceed with consciousness*. It is a full-time job to caretake this gift of life we have. Every thought, every action, every word we say is an act of creation, a choice to set grace into motion—or not.

Grace

Think of the grace of Protection as a type of light-filled net that heaven drops over you, repelling psychic free radicals—negative energy that inevitably inspires negative actions, channeling itself into collective negative acts of creation—from attaching to your energy field. The power of grace expresses itself in your life in ways seen and unseen. You may never know the many ways this grace has maneuvered you through your day, or guided the order of your thoughts, or kept a negative narrative from activating in you. I always remind people that most of us walk through our lives so unconsciously that we cannot recall the clothing we wore two days ago or what we ate four meals ago. If we cannot recall the obvious experiences of our life, chances are we'll miss the subtle divine ones most of the time.

Grant me the grace of Protection, Lord, from the darkness I cannot see in this world, as well as from the darkness of my own pride and arrogance. No wonder we fear that pride comes before a fall. You've designed us, Lord, to fall to our knees for our own Protection in the face of evil. And how perfect: that is where we always find You waiting.

21

KEEP *Me* MINDFUL *of* THIS TIME

Prayer

LORD, I CAN SO EASILY SLIP into the wasteland of darkness these days. I have felt at times as though goodness, love, hope, and our higher nature are losing the battle—and the human experience does feel like a battle some days. I know there is no such thing as a perfect nation or a perfect world, so I am not waiting or praying for perfection. I long ago stopped saying prayers that could not be answered. Expecting a perfect world is not the way to prove the existence of God. We are not perfect creatures—but paradoxically, Lord, *our design is perfect.* We have the power within us—intellectually, emotionally, creatively—to create this world to be a place of peace and equality. All we have to do is reside in sacred consciousness; cease fearing that if others have more, we will have less; and recognize that we are all woven together as part of one life force—that there is only one divine source. How utterly simple, Lord. Why do we keep retreating into cravings for more things, more control, and more superiority? Not one of those goals will extend a human life for one extra minute. Sometimes I erupt with anger and rage at people who have become insulated and refuse to see the larger picture of what is unfolding now—and then I realize that my anger is an expression of my own sense of superiority. I do not want to respond that way to people, and yet I sometimes still do. I want people to see the whole cosmic orchestra with You as the conductor, and to hear the celestial symphony in their souls. I find that I need to remind myself several times a day of the mystical truth that *the cosmic wheels of change are shifting the direction of the human experience itself.* What a time to be alive. It is easy to retreat into darkness, forgetting how light and darkness always dance together, around us and within us. Yet, when I reflect upon the perfection of our design, Lord, I am nearly awe-struck by how powerful a single act of choice is and how much a single person can do to better the lives of others. Perhaps it is enough to hear one note from Your cosmic orchestra. A celestial note, heard in the soul, chimes like no other sound in the physical world. How utterly amazing—a sound only my soul can hear. The sound of You.

Guidance

We have never known a time of such great change. Everything is experiencing transformation—from our ecology to our biology to our technology to the health of our world community. We cannot keep up with the speed of change. And nothing is as frightening to us as change. No wonder there is so much fear in the air! So many people want to go back to the way things used to be, to simpler times. But evolution never moves backward. Everything in us tells us that becoming whole, one with all creation, is the next great spiritual mountain we must climb. Our inner nature, our perfect design, already knows this truth. We feel the power of this truth in our biology now—knowing that we must treat the whole of ourselves or we do not heal. But we also learn each day that becoming a whole person is a rigorous undertaking. Imagine that this is the collective challenge we are living through in this time in history. It is no surprise we find chaos everywhere.

Grace

The grace of Mindfulness keeps us alert and aware of God in the small details in our lives. We need this grace when tasks in life depend upon our being especially mindful, like caring for a vulnerable person or taking on the arduous task of self-healing. We need this grace when we have made the decision to challenge an addiction or break free of a dark attitude.

Lord, keep me in the grace of Mindfulness.
Keep me alert to when I might slip or start to talk myself into
something I should not be doing. Keep me mindful of my own
mind games—and grant me the strength to not give in.

22

IN *the* COMPANY *of* ALL LIFE

Prayer

SOME THOUGHTS, LORD, ARE SMALL. Others are cosmic in size. I had a cosmic epiphany today, Lord: that I require the energy—the breath—of all other living creatures to sustain me. Suddenly, instantly, I felt gratitude and vulnerability colliding within me. From inside this cosmic lens, I experienced the whole fabric of life as a living, breathing organism moving through and with me. The sensation lasted for just a microsecond, but it felt as if the observational lens through which I had always looked had shattered. I was no longer an observer of life but a particle participating in the energetics of creation. I will admit to You, Lord, that I wanted to dwell in that perception—that mystical realm—for a while longer. I felt as if I was experiencing the breathing apparatus of creation itself—instead of just looking as an outsider at the flowers in the garden once they have bloomed. My mind cannot comprehend this experience. I am learning, Lord, that some experiences belong only to the soul. I believe You graced me today, Lord, by allowing me to melt for a microsecond into the truth that all life breathes together. Life would be so much less fearful if people could only glimpse the power of that truth.

Guidance

The great spiritual teachers tell us that we are all one, that what is in one is in the whole. Experiencing the power of that truth, or any truth, is like getting illuminated with pure light. In one blast, your observational understanding of life is swept away, replaced by an experience of life that is mystical. You cannot really *comprehend* that we are all interconnected. The concept sounds good in theory. It may even make sense when you contemplate that the laws of nature govern all living creatures. But when you keep a truth as theory, you have the option of debating it or denying it. Once you *experience* a truth, that truth transforms you. Its power escorts you into a new realm. You understand the intimate weave of this web of sacred life—every atom of which is conscious and holy. In our hearts, we know all of life is sacred because all of life is an expression of the Divine. That truth is embedded in the soul's DNA. We are made from the substance of that truth.

Grace

The grace of Clarity expresses itself in so many ways, one of which is to see clearly beyond the illusion of form. The Buddha gave the world the profound truth that our physical senses are easily deceived by what we see, hear, taste, smell, or touch. Nothing is as it appears to be. We cannot see the invisible network of grace or the web of life that connects all of us. Yet when we enter a quiet place of reflection, we can sense that connection within our soul. We were born knowing that all life breathes together.

Lord, grant me the grace of Clarity, especially when the illusions that allow me to believe for a moment that I am not a part of the whole slip into my mind. Help me see clearly that all life breathes with me.

23

ON *the* NATURE *of* GOD

Prayer

THERE IS NO SUCH THING as the mystical order of life and death, is there, Lord? Illness in a loved one would be so much easier to bear if illness only happened to the aged. But illness just happens. Like so many others, I have tried to decode the logic behind why we humans break down suddenly, or in the prime of life. Is it too much negativity? Too much sorrow? Not enough exercise? And then we turn to You and ask, "What is the lesson?" I now believe little of that matters. At the end of the day, the length of our lives is a cosmic decision and what power we have is best directed to quality-control choices: What is it we choose to do with the gift of life we have been given? We can abuse this gift, and consequently others, with the choices we make. Or we can appreciate this gift and share the talents of our life with others, hopefully enhancing their lives. We have been taught by the great masters that what goes around indeed comes around. If we invest grace and love in our lives, grace and love are returned a hundred times. That investment pays off in ways we cannot calculate. Perhaps one of them is that our health is indeed enhanced. And again, I have witnessed good people suffering. I suspect that You, Lord, will never be understood with Earth logic or by simple observation. We must make our choices based upon what it is we believe to be true and of value. But I have learned that our soul keeps tabs on the choices we make and notes the consequences of our actions in our blood and bones. We are permitted to forget all the good things we do, but rarely can we forget the negative. Somehow dark choices, especially those that harm others, gnaw away at our conscience like termites chomping away at dead wood. *Why is that?* I wonder. Perhaps because every choice we make really does matter.

Even if we cannot see why or how. Ultimately, I must make my choices based on my covenant with You, and how much I value the gift of this life.

Guidance

We would all like to find a way to break the cosmic code, to figure out how to talk the Divine into a private set of rules. We'd like to prevent the unknown from happening and chaos from striking. Yet no human being in the history of humanity has succeeded at this quest. It is we who must bow to the governing rules of this Universe. Though it may seem as if chaos lacks order—and that death is cruel and capricious—both are illusions. Chaos is divine reordering. The cycle of death and rebirth is the nature of life itself. We are the only species that cannot accept that cycle, for reasons of love and grief. If only we could accept that nothing we do has the power to make us exceptions to life's rules, perhaps we could focus more on what is immortal in us. That is, instead of pouring our energy into constantly trying to manipulate the laws of change, and to quell our need for control over the physical elements of our life, imagine how liberating it would feel to surrender those survival fears and accept our limitations. Pray and follow your guidance—and don't expect to be rewarded for doing so. A deep sense of trust, comfort, and acceptance gradually energizes within you as you grow into the rhythm of praying, trusting, acting, and accepting.

Grace

In the Serenity Prayer we ask to "accept the things that cannot be changed." Acceptance is a powerful grace, a soothing grace that can offset the anxiety that arises when we are up against the forces of life itself. One of the worst feelings in the world is powerlessness. Many obstacles in life remind us that we are indeed powerless to stop what is unfolding around us, no matter how much we would have it be otherwise. Acceptance is a holy remedy for the anxiety that rises in us during times like that. It reminds us to "Let go and let God" once we have done all that we can do.

Grant me the grace of Acceptance, Lord, most especially
when I am in the midst of circumstances beyond my control and
those that are difficult for me to accept. I cannot bear to see people
hurt. I find the suffering of children incomprehensible. Nothing about
the darkness of humanity is acceptable to me. And yet, humanity is
not going to change overnight because I cannot bear that darkness.
So I must accept that, even in the midst of the darkest act, heaven is
bearing witness. That is a truth I do accept. With that truth I can
feel the calm of grace tranquilizing my self-inflicted chaos.

24

LIVING *in* EXPECTANCY

Prayer

I FELT SOMETHING DIFFERENT in the air today, but what was it? And was the "it" actually "in the air"? I spent the early hours of this day as I always spend my mornings—wrapped in silence—only today I felt as if I were waiting for something. But what? Grabbing my coffee, I made my way to the porch for my morning conversation with you, Lord. And then I knew. I was expecting You, but not in the usual way of our morning quiet time. I am now accustomed to the deep silence of the morning. By habit I drift off into mystical contemplation. I crave this inner time of holy silence. But today I felt as if I were expecting a guest. And then I wondered for a brief second—had I been sent a message? Did it require deep stillness to be retrieved? No. Sometime during these early morning hours, Lord, I realized—and perhaps that was the message—that the grace of expectancy was flooding into my atmosphere. The only thing asked of me was to breathe it in.

Guidance

What is it we expect from God? Perhaps nothing. And then again, perhaps everything. Every person has a unique theology. I do not expect rewards for good behavior or protection from difficulties because I was generous to someone. Heaven does not keep score like that. But I do expect—or rather, deeply believe—that all prayers are answered. I do not expect, however, to understand *how* they are answered. Nor do I expect to have prayers answered as *I* would want them to be answered. I just know they are answered. Sometimes we get to see the changes brought about through the grace of prayer, but many times we do not. Maybe our soul in some way exists in a constant state of anticipating the company of the sacred. Our soul recognizes that sparkle of divine light. When it arrives, our imagination erupts into expectancy: that blissful state of being in which we are flooded with the awareness that all wonders are somehow really possible. And that state of blissful wonder is perhaps the purest state of expectancy.

Grace

Expectancy is not a grace many are familiar with, though everyone is familiar with having expectations. Expectancy, however, is the exact opposite of what it means to have expectations. Having expectations means you are living in the assumption that you are owed something—a particular outcome, or a good time, or perhaps a healing—because you paid a certain sum of money, or you signed a contract, or because, well, you are just *you*. The grace of Expectancy, on the other hand, fills you with an inner sensation of endless wondrous possibilities. Expectancy feels as if you are about to implode with creativity, the pure vibration of life itself. This grace is not given as a reward for anything. It is a grace that illuminates your love of life. It highlights the endless possibilities of the gift of life. This grace inspires us to recognize that our life is filled with creative possibilities.

Lord, I ask for the blessing of the grace of Expectancy.
Rather than show me directions and outcomes—prayers I realize
come from fear—let me feel the power of my potential bursting
inside me, illuminating my creative nature. What, then,
should I expect from myself? Anything is possible.

25

COMMENTS on a MIRACLE

Prayer

LORD, I LISTENED TO A WOMAN TODAY tell me she experienced a miracle. She said she was healed of cancer. She said she prayed for a healing and You heard her prayers. She was overwhelmed with gratitude and joy and the desire to share her miracle story with everyone who would listen. She told me she did not have much faith before her cancer. And now she deeply believes in You. I asked her what made her turn to prayer when she did not have a prayer life prior to her diagnosis of stage 4 cancer. She said that her doctor told her that she had essentially run out of medical options and that all she could do now was pray. And so, she did just that. She prayed for divine intervention. She told me that the experience of nearly dying with cancer changed her completely. Assuming she was going to die, she gave away most of her belongings, noting how eagerly some people wanted her stuff. She told me that as she saw people so familiar to her going through her personal belongings, she realized she was not going to be missed at all by some of them. Their lives would go on just fine without her. Others wept inconsolably. Lord, I think this lovely woman was given many miracles, the least of which was the recovery of her health. She spoke like a cosmic traveler, not wanting to burden her new life with the physical and emotional baggage from the last part of her journey. She wants to know only about the power of her inner life and what she can do—while she is still here—to make the world a better place. She said her cancer was well worth the price of liberating her from her previous life. That transformation is what she considers the real miracle.

Guidance

Again and again I witness that we truly do not know the genuine core of our suffering. Like blaming the boiling water when we poured the hot water too fast out of the pot and splashed ourselves, we want to place the blame somewhere else. But the truth is, our carelessness was the reason we got burned. Perhaps we were distracted, or tense, or angry. For a split second, those fracturing emotions had more control over our balance than our common sense. We can treat the burn, but does ointment heal anger or anxiety? The healing we require is at a much deeper level—the level where our fears reside. Though a burn—or cancer—may cause severe suffering, the inner suffering of the soul is often far more debilitating, in ways that are hidden even to the patient. We are often the last to know what it is about ourselves that requires the most healing.

Grace

Humility is a grace not often associated with healing, and yet it is the grace most required to heal. We are never on the receiving end of our own behavior. We never see fear or panic wash over our own faces. Perhaps that is why these intense emotions are felt so keenly within our physical body. Illness makes us vulnerable, and often in that vulnerability we cannot clearly see what it is that needs healing within us. We look for the obvious because we want illness and healing to follow the formula of one solution for one problem. But healing does not follow formulas. Healing is a mystical journey, one that requires encounters with truth and a process of self-reflection. In the pursuit of your own healing, for example, you should not seek to know "Who scared me?" Rather, ask yourself, "Why am I so afraid?" Only answers to the second question will free you from fear—and that is ultimately the greatest healing of all.

*Lord, grant me the grace of Humility in order that I may
see myself clearly. Fear brings out the worst in me—my hubris
and anger. No illness can truly be healed when I am filled with hubris.
That is more toxic to my healing than any disease. Grant me
Humility, Lord, and the capacity to act on that grace.*

26

THE ATMOSPHERE *of* MIRACLES

Prayer

I WAS WONDERING this morning, Lord, does heaven have a limit on the number of miracles one person is allowed to experience in one life? I've witnessed a few miraculous healings. I am well past doubting that You intervene in our lives. And I have spent time with people who have experienced miraculous healings. I will admit that I was curious—why them? How could I not be curious? If I did come up with conclusions about the way of heaven, if such a thing were possible at all, I concluded that there is no pattern to the blessing of a miracle. A miracle can happen any time, any place, to anyone. Heaven doesn't play favorites, I've gathered. But in my little quest to crack open this mystery, I also concluded that healing is but one of many ways the messengers of heaven are sent to intervene in our lives. Life is a theater, set up for divine intervention to occur all the time. The common thread I found in all the people who experienced healings is that they were expecting You at any moment. It did not occur to them that You would not show up, even though they were not necessarily anticipating that their illness would be completely healed. But some form of assistance to them—or their family—would be given. And they were open to whatever grace You poured into their lives. One person told me, "I always expect God." What a powerful prayer— always expect God. And so, I will.

Guidance

People who have experienced divine intervention directly— aka a miracle—have illuminated souls. They no longer doubt the presence of God in their lives or the power of prayer. They radiate faith. You can feel their faith vibrating around them, pure fearlessness. No one can imagine this consciousness; you either embody it or you do not. We are heat-seeking missiles when it comes to divine light. We crave this pure light as much, if not more, than we crave pure air and water. It is sustenance for our soul. We stare hard at beautiful sunrises and sunsets, hoping to engage a microsecond of sacred illumination. We read poetry and scale mountains and sojourn to sacred sites, carrying a private agenda in our heart: maybe, just maybe, we will have an encounter with the sacred in that place. Who does not want to encounter even the slightest contact with something greater than themselves, something truly miraculous?

Grace

The grace of Expectancy, yet again. This time, think of this grace as a bright light you carry within you, always keeping a place ready for a mystical visitation. Live in expectation of holy intervention at all times. Imagine that your life is an atmosphere, perfectly attuned to support the miraculous. You do not require catastrophes or suffering for divine intervention. Inspiration and direct guidance are equally mystical, miraculous experiences.

Lord, I always expect You.

27

A REQUEST *for* DIVINE INTERVENTION

Prayer

LORD, I RECEIVED A CALL today from someone asking for prayers. She is suffering horribly. In moments like this, I have to remind myself that You know the content of my prayers and who I am now praying for. I know better than to ask for specifics. Since the content of my heart is not hidden from Your view, I admit I am tempted to ask. But I have learned—and I continue to learn—that I do not know what is best for another person. I do not know if You are calling her home, if this is the closure of her life. The mystery of life never ceases to grip my attention. I have seen some people recover from terminal illnesses at the last minute—one person after receiving the last rites. I know You sent an angel from Your healing realm to deliver that healing grace. Even the physician said the recovery was a miracle. Perhaps our time to depart from life is negotiable after all. I do not know. I *do* know that I am asking for the grace of mercy to be given to this woman. Please let that grace flow abundantly through her and upon her family. I know mercy is a grace that, like a mustard seed, can bring down an obstacle we consider a mountain in our lives. I am asking for mercy, Lord, upon this family. Maybe with mercy, they will be able to forgive what they think of as unforgivable. It is not You who needs to be merciful, Lord. It is *we* who are without mercy far too often. We are blind to the consequences of having a merciless heart. Mercy is a grace poured into the human heart, *for* the human heart. So, grant them mercy, Lord. For I know the healing power of that grace.

Guidance

One day while deep in prayer, I understood that God does not require mercy; we do. I have never met a person who has said to me, "I am riddled with pain because I have lived a merciless life." Yet a person without mercy finds cruelty effortless and can rationalize inhumane decisions. Such people reside in the illusion that they exist separate from the whole, that somehow their actions toward others will not have consequences in their own lives. We pray for others both intimately and at a distance, reminding ourselves that we do not know what is unfolding in their lives.

Grace

Mercy is a powerful grace, one that opens the heart to the hearts of others. Long ago, people prayed for Mercy daily, knowing that their lives were so fragile in the world. Our *inner* lives are now the fragile landscape. We are discovering, together, how easy it is to be overwhelmed by this journey of life. We need to be merciful with each other.

Lord, have Mercy upon me, that I may also be merciful to others. Let the grace of Mercy reside in my heart, especially when judgment of others arises. I do not want to be a person carrying cruelty in my heart. I would rather feel the grace of Mercy flow through me— and receive Mercy in my weakest moments in return.

28

THE PRESENCE of ANGELS

Prayer

SOMETIMES, LORD, I CAN sense that I have stepped into the presence of angels. I cannot see Your holy messengers, yet I know they are near—very near. Someone asked me once, "How do you know an angel is near? What does the presence of an angel feel like?" Some questions have no answers. I could see that he wanted a reply that held a secret ingredient, a code perhaps. This man struck me as a grown-up child, longing to somehow find a way to encounter the sacred. If only he could glimpse the wing of an angel, the mere flutter of proof that the invisible world is filled with benevolent guardians of light, he would be able to believe. I do not know how to penetrate that wall of doubt in people, Lord. But I constantly see the consequences of that barrier in their lives. I know this world is filled with angels. They are constantly watching over their assigned human beings . . . if we only knew, if we only knew. If people could realize, in the moment of fear or confusion, that assistance was hovering right next to them, what comfort that would bring. And yet, people do not understand the *way* of Divine assistance. Angels have a noninterference policy. It took me a long time, Lord, to truly understand that guidance is their task, whereas ours is choice. The choice before us is whether to trust the power of the sacred realm to guide us when we cannot yet see or to fight our way through events that have already occurred. Everything in the physical world has already occurred, at least from heaven's perspective. It is a mystical truth that anything we see in the physical world is already history. It took me a long time to truly grasp that the stuff of the physical world is the *end product* of our collective choices, not the beginning. But I am grasping this truth, Lord, little by little. If we base our choices on what we see, we are responding to what has already happened. Real change begins in the invisible world . . . and it starts with listening to the guidance of our angels. What is required of us is learning to trust the voice of our soul. I have to add, Lord, that I would not mind if every now and again my angel screamed instead of whispered.

Guidance

Trust is a grace for a reason. We cannot thrive, much less survive, without it. No relationship can be sustained without trust. And what of trusting ourselves? If you do not trust yourself, you cannot trust another person—ever. You will not trust that people love you, or that they will keep their word to you. The absence of trust has created the litigious society we now reside in. Litigiousness is a psychic epidemic that is causing more suffering than can be measured. At its core is the fear of one's natural capacity to receive intuitive instructions from holy messengers. We have become a society attracted to the idea of angels for entertainment, for theatrical guidance around business decisions and personal relationships. Which is nonsense, if not sacrilege. Angelic guidance is directed at assisting you in the management of your conscience, in making decisions weighing what is good or evil, right or wrong, or in the best interests of other human beings. Angels are tasked with guarding the path of your soul—not your occupation or love life. And in matters of your soul, you can trust their guidance to be the truth.

Grace

Trust is one of our most essential graces. You may know you are suffering from the absence of Trust—that you have "trust issues." But perhaps you have never recognized that you are, quite simply, out of grace. And that is a spiritual crisis, not just a personal one. You can get all the therapy you want, but Trust me on this: no amount of therapy will heal the absence of Trust. That requires an infusion of the grace itself. And for that, you require prayer.

Grant me the grace of Trust, Lord, to not fear the voice of my soul. I know that voice is my lifeline to You, and that to sense it even once means I can never deny it again. Grant me the grace of Trust, Lord, that I might begin with trusting my inner self. Then, little by little, I will find my way to You.

29

CONVERSATION *with an* ATHEIST

Prayer

I HAD AN ENCOUNTER WITH an atheist the other day, Lord. He asked me to explain all the evil in the world. Not just some of the evil, mind you, but *all* the evil. Evil was his argument for Your nonexistence. Lord, honestly, why do I encounter these people? I swear . . . to God . . . that *You* set up these situations for me. This guy came at me, guns blazing, saying that if there *were* a God, then all the catastrophes in the world would not happen. Children wouldn't suffer and horrible people would not be in political office. (I have to admit, Lord, that I was tempted to agree with that last comment of his . . . but only for a moment.) While he was going down his list, Lord, I had a flashback to my childhood, to a time when I had the same thoughts. *Why don't You just wipe out all these bad people?* I remember thinking when I was nine years old. *You could just vacuum them all off the planet and the rest of us would wake up the next morning and all would be well.* Solutions to human behavior seemed so simple then. At that age I even considered that You might *use* my ideas! So when this man finally exhausted his list of evils, he asked me why You allowed them. I asked him if he had told a lie that day. I added that if he did not answer the question truthfully, that itself qualified as an act of evil. He pulled back in his chair and stared at me, but he didn't answer—leaving me to assume that he had told at least one lie so far that day. I added that lying was his contribution to evil that day. Since I did not know the gravity of his lie—that is, how many people it had impacted— he could be seriously in league with evil or still just negotiating terms. I added that people do not want to believe in God because it helps them anesthetize their own consciences. In turn, acts of evil explode all over the place. Evil has human fingerprints all over it. I don't recall who left the table first, Lord, but I suspect You followed him home.

Guidance

We question the existence of God—or deny it entirely—because that position allows us to "talk about God" but does not commit us to acting with our conscience engaged. I emphasize the word *conscience*. Our conscience is wired to our intuitive system. Detaching from the sacred realm deadens our connection to conscience, and consequently we can no longer intuit what is good and what is evil. We get to decide what suits us so far as good and evil are concerned. But that is itself evil. Some things in life and nature are inherently evil—regardless of what our spiritual beliefs are. It doesn't matter whether you're an atheist or a believer. It will always be wrong—in my language, a *sin*—to murder someone, or to set up another person to suffer so you do not. It will always be a sin to abuse a child. And in our human DNA, we know that. We morph ourselves into a monster species when we decide that we can reorder the Universe—and the nature of good and evil—to suit our personal preferences. There is a power greater than us governing life. That power is fundamentally sacred, and it is expressed through the laws of the Universe. If we break those laws, we pay the price. Simple as that. It is in our best interest to "humble up" and become spiritually law-abiding humans.

Grace

Humility is the best grace ever. You can't go wrong holding in your heart the reminder to humble up. Position yourself in front of photos sent back to Earth from the Hubble telescope, and ask yourself if you are really qualified to redesign the order of the whole Universe. I think not. Since forever, the balance of polarities has ordered the cycles of life. Darkness and light, masculine and feminine, right and wrong, yes and no, good and bad. The law of balance—not denial—is key to our well-being. We must learn to balance these polarities within us. Each polarity represents the nature of the Divine in its full spectrum. We have dark potential and we have light potential. We must choose in each moment whether to engage our light or our shadow. And together, we reside in the sum of our choices—the human experience.

Lord, I see this Universe most accurately when I look through humble eyes. Remind me when I start redesigning the Universe to suit my own behavior that I am way out of my creative league. I will humble up and remind myself again—and again—to walk gently on this Earth, this holy ground of Your making.

30

SHARING BLESSINGS

Prayer

I REALIZED THIS MORNING as I sat in prayer time with you, Lord, that I always feel blessed. I always have. And then I thought, *What exactly is the feeling of a blessing?* I closed my eyes for a moment to see if I could enter into the grace of a blessing. I felt utter lightness, but it was more than that. I felt *holy companionship*, the presence of grace surrounding me. Somehow it communicated the comforting message that all is as it should be. All is watched, all is known. In that light, the difficulties that those I love and I are facing appear resolvable, as if a sacred support team is already waiting for us at the finish line. Lord, the light of blessing cannot be described; it is a mystical substance. But it can be shared, even silently, through prayer for others. There is no end to the light. It never fades or runs out of power. Today I will pause continually to think of someone whom I surround in *blessing light*. I don't know how Your side of things works, but I do know that prayers are delivered. I imagine a shaft of light opening over the person I'm praying for, shining into his or her life. The light of blessing is not just "ordinary light"—I know that. Divine light is filled with particles of active sacredness, holy life substance. But these words are just words. I recognize this holy light because it is the only light that leaves me with the sensation of fearlessness. Nothing in my life feels insurmountable or frightening with this light— how could I not want to share such a blessing with others? Especially when I recognize how much suffering comes from imagined fears—all of which evaporate in a split second in the presence of this light.

Guidance

Each one of us needs to find a way to survive in this world. Survival is the initial stage in our development toward selfhood. It brings out every fear we have—financial, social, food, relationships. Think for a moment on how much time you spend consumed with matters related to your safety and security. Could there be a greater blessing than to defeat the authority survival fears have over you? Grace—or divine intervention—does not work like fictional magic, ensuring your earthly security. Contrary to what so many people would like to think. Grace aims its influence at your soul, empowering you to confront your own fears, once and for all.

Grace

The grace of Blessing pours into our lives all the time. Do not look for Blessings to come in packages. They are interior gifts, soul gifts. And in turn, you express those gifts in your life. *You* are the agent of change in your life, utilizing graces given to you. Sometimes you are blessed with insights or wisdom. Or—imagine this—you are given the blessing of an illness so you do not make choices that would lead you down a dark karmic path. Blessings come in so many unexpected forms that most of us have no idea.

Lord, help me see my life's journey as the story of blessings unfolding one day at a time. And help me keep my eyes and heart open, to bless others along the way. My life would be a long and empty journey were it not for all of those I love. Let the blessings that come to me come through me as well. Let them shower those who already reside in my heart, and those in need whom I have yet to love.

31

ENTERING QUIETUDE

Prayer

I HAVE GROWN SO ACCUSTOMED to a quiet life, Lord. I am not even aware any longer that I live in a soundless environment until something loud disrupts my world. I find noise oppressive and even painful. Mind you, Lord, I would ask that You spare me from becoming hypersensitive to the world in which I dwell. I refuse to become someone who has to avoid this or that, except out of my own choice. I choose silence because it suits my creative nature. I love the way it feels. I love the softness of silent air and the gentleness of quietude. I love that the air around me is not vibrating with noise. I can relax my listening skills, turning them inward instead of remaining attuned to external input. Sometimes I sense that a message has been delivered to my soul, that unmistakable sensation that I have just experienced a whisper from heaven. Those messages fill my soul with . . . with what? With—*everything*. Some whispers are not even words—just feathers of light dropped into my soul. Teresa of Ávila wrote that if God gets into the wall of your soul for even a second, it's enough for a lifetime. I bow to that truth.

Guidance

Everyone seeks divine guidance, even when they do not know it. We are all searching for holy reinforcement. It is in our nature to seek resolution. When we pause to wonder, *What is happening here?* or *How do I resolve this chaos?* we are seeking counsel from our soul. We are seeking advice beyond the limitations of our confused minds. We are in search of quietude, a repose from the madness created by the reactive decisions we make out of fear. Clarity arises in quietude, which is more than a retreat into a private room. Quietude emerges from within. Like a tranquilizing breeze, it anesthetizes the confusing voices shouting in your mind. Quietude penetrates into your nervous system, calming the panic you feel. Your situation reshapes itself and the message is clear: You can handle this. All will be well.

Grace

The grace of Counsel is unmistakable. It is visceral. Divine Counsel is not advice. You are not being given an opinion. Divine Counsel comes in many forms, be it what to say to someone else or personal Counsel—sensing a *knowingness* deep in your solar plexus that all will be well. Knowingness, an odd word for everyday use, is a mystical tool—a means through which the Divine speaks to us. We experience an immediate shift in consciousness. One minute we do not know, and suddenly there is a sense of absolute confidence. It is not a rational or logical experience. Knowingness is not backed up by facts or data. It is an experience validated by the immediate empowerment you sense that eradicates all insecurities.

Lord, I must first learn to recognize how it is that I create my own chaos, how much my own fears influence my choices. Grant me moments of quietude, that I may receive Your Counsel. Guide me to penetrate through my own insecurities and the power they have to influence all that I create in my life.

32

WHAT IS HAPPINESS?

Prayer

I AM ALWAYS ASKED ABOUT HOW to find happiness. One day—suddenly, just like that—the question struck me as preposterous. *Find* happiness? I recall telling myself to be mindful of the look I had on my face. I know that I am prone to expressing all over my face exactly what I am thinking (although I am getting better at monitoring myself). I did the only thing I could do in that moment, Lord. I prayed to You: "You'd better download me some badass compassion real fast because I am in need of it." Why did I get so irritated? The question seemed so meaningless to me. But after I prayed, I felt an overwhelming need to look the questioner directly in her eyes. When I did, waves of her loneliness pierced my heart. I knew You had answered my prayer. I felt her emptiness so deeply it damn near broke my heart. We sat for a while and I asked her about her life. Not surprisingly, her story was long and lonely. And here's a word my soul hit me with: harmless. Her story was harmless. This woman was gentle. She was consciously walking the Earth with the intention of doing no harm. Compassion was breaking her heart, and I saw that. She was in desperate need of soul companions—at least one. I paused for a moment and asked inwardly whether compassion and happiness were destined to do battle in the human heart—breaking it and opening it by turns. I found I wanted her to be surrounded with, well, *happiness*. So I finally said the only thing that occurred to me. I told her to stop being disappointed in herself. To stop telling herself that she wasn't doing enough to make the world a better place. To stop telling herself that she wasn't *enough*. Just stop the self-torment. Happiness begins when torment ends.

Guidance

We don't *find* happiness. We *become* it. We *embody* it. We decide to see our life through a different lens. We cease telling ourselves that we should be somewhere else—that "other" place we will never actually get to. There is no greener grass; it's the lawn we are standing on that we must water and care for. Happiness begins the second we stop believing it is somewhere other than here. And then, no matter where we want to go, it comes along with us.

Grace

The grace of Compassion is powerful stuff. Compassion doesn't open your heart. It *takes over* your heart—and it never leaves. Compassion is one of those graces that can hurt the carrier unless it is correctly used. The pain of others is too much to carry unless you do something to lessen their burden. I give that to you as a warning. Compassion is meant to be used, not stored.

---

*Lord, I cannot ask for Compassion from others unless
I am willing to be compassionate myself. I cannot expect to receive
in this life what I am not willing to give. I do not think of myself as
someone in need of Compassion, but I have no idea what tomorrow
may bring. I do not know what challenges I might face that may
bring me to my knees, literally and figuratively. So please open
my heart to this holy grace, that I may realize that the
suffering of others is, in some way, my own.*

33

A MOMENT *of* GRACE

Prayer

I OBSERVED AN ARGUMENT TODAY while walking through the park. It was nasty. A man and a woman were raging at each other, their anger and pain flowing out of their mouths like arrows on fire. He stormed away, and his last and very loud words to her were that he wanted out of their marriage. She sat on a bench and sobbed. He had just ended their marriage. You know, Lord, in moments like that, nothing can be said—and yet, that does not mean nothing can be done. So often people have said to me, "But what can I do?" or "Someone should do something." Helplessness flashes all over them. They withdraw into the child archetype, fully expecting the "adults" in their world to carry their responsibility for them. *Others will clean up the planet. Others will take care of the poor. Others will make the world a better place. I am only one person. I am exhausted with the helplessness of so many people.* We humans are many things, but helpless is not one of them. It wasn't my place to invade that woman's pain at the park. But I could send out a prayer for guidance, and I did: "Do You want me to do something for her?" I felt the instruction "Sit near her and release grace." I sat on the next bench, closed my eyes, and let grace do its healing work. I didn't expect to open my eyes and see her smiling. Grace is not fairy dust. But I knew she had received a message, a deep knowing. That no matter the oncoming storm she now had to navigate through, she would be fine. She would not be demolished. She was not as weak or fragile as she thought. She may have imagined herself as strong before; now perhaps she knew she had no choice but to believe in herself. Grace does not reveal outcomes or assurances of how anything will work out. Everything unfolds according to *our* choices. Grace assures us that when moments of choice do arise, we will somehow be able to rely upon ourselves to make decisions that might even surprise us.

Guidance

We really require so little to change the course of our lives. We don't need money or another college degree or a crew of people behind us. We need only to believe in ourselves and in the integrity of our own choices. Self-integrity and personal power will not clear the obstacles from our path. But such inner power gives us the stamina to stick to that path, regardless of the obstacles that come our way.

Grace

Wholeness is probably an unfamiliar grace to you, and yet we need this grace more than ever. We now live in the age in which "becoming whole" is a living command within our soul. Everything we do, say, think, and feel has a subtle template of "wholism" built into it. We now think about our health and our body as a whole life system—one that interconnects our emotions, our intellect, our spirit, and our body. The law of wholism reveals that what is *in one* is *in the whole*, and what is *done to one* is *done to the whole*. Perceiving our world through the power and prism of Wholeness is a far greater challenge than, say, eating right. Living the law of wholism requires that you enter into the true meaning of the word. It shares a root with *holy*. The laws governing all of life are holy. All is one, and all life breathes together. The grace to become whole is, in truth, the grace to know and understand the power of all that is holy within you.

Grant me the grace to become a whole person,
Lord, to realize the power of what it means to be present
with all that is holy—within me, as well as within others. It is
easy to envision the whole of life through the lens of holiness.

34

EXPLODING *with* ANGER

Prayer

I RECOGNIZE THAT I DO not know what is really going on in this world, Lord. But even so, at times I cannot help seething with anger and rage at the brutality of human beings, at our endless greed and cruelty that harm so much of humanity. Do people really believe that more money will buy them even one more day of life? I honestly think they do; why else would they crave it so much? Will people never learn that no amount of earthly power can gain them one extra breath of life? Or help them heal a terminal illness? It's enough to send me into a self-righteous fit. So when that happens, what do I do? I have discovered that screaming at You gets me nowhere. Teresa of Ávila, my beloved saint, got exasperated too—at You, I might add. I am reminded right now that when I felt like this before, I reached for one of her books. No surprise: I managed to find that one small passage in which she voiced her frustration to You. *Just be done with us,* she told You, *or heal us.* And then she paused and noted that You had given us the most powerful of all weapons: prayer. Teresa believed that prayer was the most powerful of all tools to change our world, and to change ourselves. Oh, how she trusted You. And somehow the grace of that saint has penetrated into my soul, as if she were a guardian being of mine. I think prayer might just work like an Internet blast—except it happens on the *inner*-net, the soul grid. We can send light-filled thoughts of courage and inspiration to millions of people at the same time, none of whom have any idea. They simply feel the need to pause for a second, take a deep breath, and release a buildup of stress that would otherwise lead them to act in a negative way. And in one second, the subtle atmosphere of the world has shifted. In that way, prayer is like a spiritual homeopathic remedy. And so, I shall follow the instructions of Teresa: scream at You first and then bow my head in prayer.

Guidance

If we wait for the world around us to make sense, we will wait a very long time. The physical world will never be tranquil or peaceful, fair or just. Why? Because for some reason, we cannot resist the impulse to fight among ourselves. We cannot imagine communicating without the use of our tempers. We feel we *need* to scream at this world every now and again, if only because so much of the pain that goes on around us is so unnecessary. If ever we needed proof of the power of prayer, it should be in the fact that—given the lesser qualities of human nature and how many of us there are—we still manage to survive. We haven't yet blown ourselves up with nuclear weapons. Some power greater than ourselves must have our back.

Grace

If ever we needed the grace of Divine Intervention, it's when we feel the rumblings of anger coming on. How often have you had the experience of almost exploding—almost saying something horrible—when suddenly you hear a voice: "Careful—think twice before saying that!" or "Walk away—now!" You rarely pause and think, *Hmmm, who is talking to me?* Instead, you act on the instruction. You may not even realize that you are responding to Intervention—to guidance that is saving you from your darkest potential. If you follow that advice, inevitably you will remember it later. *I am so grateful I didn't say what I almost said. Thank God I walked out that door!* Similarly those who did *not* listen—caving instead to their darkest impulses—may count that moment among their deepest lifetime regrets. The grace of Divine Intervention expresses itself through such encounters; a word or a phrase erupts directly into your intended negative action and suddenly you're rerouted. Your worst impulses don't get played out, and later you look back with gratitude and wonder.

Lord, prevent me from acting on my worst instincts,
especially when I am most out of control. Heighten my senses
so I recognize those holy sparks of Divine Intervention so that
I may pause and listen more deeply to the other person, not
overreact from fear, and make decisions from wisdom.

35

THE DARK SIDE *of* CREATION

Prayer

SO YOU ANSWERED MY QUESTION about the power of prayer through a dream, a nocturnal visitation with a demon. I have never doubted—not once in my life—that prayer was power, Lord. But this dream showed me how grace and our prayers work together, and why we must pray. I did not realize that the power of our collective prayers flows through the governing mystical laws of creation, that in this way it influences physical actions unfolding on the Earth. Every positive human action generates grace, just as a prayer does. Every action is accounted for in one way or another—an action is generated either through positive or negative intention. In my dream I saw the demon in myself laugh. I witnessed the race between grace and hatred. Hatred was collecting psychic free radicals and flushing them through a cosmic-sized burning volcano. Hot, melting lava poured forth into the psychic fields of millions and millions of human beings, intensifying their fears and destroying their grounded sense of humanity. At the same time, grace poured a cool, sparkling remedy upon the masses, attempting to sooth the consuming fires. Alas, the lava was moving faster than the supply of grace. "I've won already," the demon said as he began closing the door of hell in my face. Even in my dream, I thought, *Just like you . . . just like you to claim a victory you have not yet won.*

Guidance

Evil relies upon the weak side of human nature: fear, arrogance, vulnerability, and the disbelief in evil itself—in its presence and power in our lives. But the light has a few advantages that are cosmic sized. Evil never drafts brave people; the light *always* does. Evil is attracted to cowards, for they are the most controllable. Their souls are the most easily consumed. Brave, prayerful people do not negotiate their values or their character. They are useless to evil; they will not become minions. Greedy, weak, needy people who have no sense of self-esteem, on the other hand, are prime candidates for evil's schemes. They have yet to even value themselves, much less others, so they are people who can be bought for dollars. They will say and do anything for money and power. And most of all, these are the people who cannot afford to believe in evil. If they did they would have to take down every mirror in their homes.

Grace

The grace of Protection is real, and it is essential. Just as we need Protection in so many ways from the dangers in the physical world, we also need Protection from the influences of the subtle realm. All the great spiritual masters knew this truth. Our worst enemies are invisible: our fears and the fears of others; our weaknesses; and the dark inner narratives we often tell ourselves that are not true. Everyone needs the grace of Protection. Picture yourself in a castle and think of this grace as the power to haul up the drawbridge.

Lead me not into temptation, but deliver me from evil.
Keep me from dark influences that I cannot myself see. Hover
over me, Lord, day and night. Keep me in a field of Your grace,
and hold me as closely as You hold goodness and light—
safe from the darkness that surely resides on the Earth.

36

WONDERING *out* LOUD, LORD

Prayer

SO MUCH HELP IS NEEDED NOW, Lord. Everywhere I look, someone needs assistance. The other day I gave money to a woman pleading for assistance while standing in the middle of the street. I said a prayer for her as I drove away. Her face was bruised, and she radiated fear and panic. I asked You then, "Did You see her? Help her, Lord. Help her." I could feel my heart racing with panic as I continued to drive home. I wanted to pull over and weep and pray and ask for a sign from You that things are going to get better—soon, fast, tomorrow. But as soon as I had that thought, the next thought dropped into me: lower, deeper, into my soul. You had responded. Transformation is a long journey, a rigorous one, and always a painful one. I know You've sent us alerts through our intuitive wiring for years that something was coming. I've had many conversations with people who have commented that they could feel change coming—climate change, or something else. But I think perhaps they never believed that something would actually happen. And so now what? I guess we work on ourselves and transform those parts that do not serve us. We become more than we are now. We share instead of hoard; love instead of hate; give instead of take. You're going to have to do some serious Divine intervening in these times ahead, Lord. Help us all through the challenges that await us. I know there will be many, and if ever there was a time when humanity needed the holy alchemy of courage and compassion, it's now.

Guidance

I know enough about the workings of heaven to know that Divine intervention occurs at that point when we have exhausted our resources, or when we find ourselves in a predicament due to our own innocence or absence of awareness. Who knows how many times we have been unknowingly saved from catastrophes. We'll never know, because heaven is an invisible ally. We will all be given plenty of opportunities to offer assistance or to ask for it in the months—and perhaps years—ahead. And in those times when we are in service to others, or are ourselves in need of others' compassion, it is the power of grace that makes that holy alchemy happen.

Grace

All graces are powerful. They are silent, mystical forces that subtly influence our life currents, always in transformational ways. Often graces blend together. Love, trust, hope, and faith are frequently woven together, as they build upon one another. Courage and Compassion likewise generate a type of holy alchemy within us, inspiring us to act in brave and bold ways for the benefit of others. Courage and Compassion are not measured by outcomes. It often takes as much Courage to help one person as it does to help a dozen or a thousand. But the holy alchemy generated by Courage and Compassion can inspire you to step out of your safe place for the sake of others, maybe for the first time in your life.

Lord, grant me the Courage and Compassion to weather
the storms spilling over into my life in these times of chaos.
Help me know how to respond, so that I can prevent myself from
running away. I need to remember again and again that all life
breathes together, that what is in one person is also in me.
Their struggles could easily be mine. So, grant me Courage and
Compassion, even when I see only calmness in front of me.

37

A CALL FOR *the* GRACES OF UNDERSTANDING *and* FORGIVENESS

Prayer

THIS EVENING, LORD, I am filled with gratitude for the grace of understanding. Because in the second I prayed for that grace, I felt it pour into me. I do not know why I meet the people I do, but I no longer question. I now assume that all of us breathe together. Desperation is unmistakable. It is one of the emotions we cannot fake or mask. Desperation has a feel—a vibration—that is unmistakable. I wonder if it's what the soul sounds like when it is screaming for help. I asked this person to tell me what the source of his suffering was, but he could not say it. I have rarely seen pain like I saw on his face, Lord. As soon as I sat with him, I felt angels surrounding us. In that subtle, sensitive field of quietude their presence brings, I went on alert. I asked him to tell me what was on his mind—and then I realized that his mind was shattered. It had become a chamber of horrors. What, I wondered, had he witnessed—or done? I asked to be given the grace of understanding, to be shown what needed to be said that I may assist him. I heard the word *death*. I asked him if he wanted to speak about death. His eyes filled with tears as he said, "No, but death keeps speaking to me. All of them." He had been a mercenary in another country, and now he was haunted by those whose lives he ended. He told me he'd had a near-death experience one night. He fell in his room, and the blow to his head knocked the life out of him long enough for him to be escorted out of his body by a being of light. I imagine, Lord, that this was your plan. He said everyone he had killed greeted him—but not with rage or anger. They came full of love—to tell him to stop killing. And he did. But now, he said, he cannot forgive himself. I told him that I needed to turn him over to You. Obviously, heaven considered him worth saving; why else would he have had such a profound encounter with the people he had harmed? As always, Lord, I thought I was with this person because I needed to help him—and it was the other way around. But then he said, "You know, you don't realize how painful hatred is until you experience love. And then you understand how you have used your hatred to do whatever you want to anyone. You don't ever have to think of anyone when you have hatred in your heart. Love, on the other hand, compels you to put others first. But even then you still have to find a way to live with all the hateful things you've done and said to so many. Not to mention what you've done to yourself. Can forgiveness really heal that level of guilt?" I told him that praying for forgiveness often worked organically—gradually lifting and refurbishing the soul—but it took time. I said his only other option was to become consumed in self-hate and remorse. I added that sometimes we need the help of others on our journey to retrieve ourselves from our own choices, to put ourselves back together again. I suggested he find that help and get on with the task, as heaven was apparently overseeing his journey.

Guidance

Every now and again, I am stunned by an encounter with another human being. Sometimes it's because of who they are, or maybe the way they behave. Often it's because of what they believe. I am accustomed to listening to people share their personal histories, and usually I'm more shocked by what has been done to them than by what they, themselves, have done. This time, however, I was not speaking to a victim of abuse. This time the perpetrator was before me. He was attempting to empty his soul of wounds so deep and horrific that he could barely bring himself to voice them. Yet this is a world in which aggressors and the aggressed, the poor and the rich, those with a voice and those without are in a continual power struggle with each other.

It is an archetypal war, one waged on multiple levels—from the physical plane to the psychic. Rich people who fear the poor rising up through education anticipate those people will eventually dilute their power and wealth. So they retreat into negative spin about them, lest love inspire them into benevolent action. Poor people see the oppression; they are not imagining it. Out of such an archetypal battlefield come mercenaries, wars, and revolutions. Divine intervention is required to break through the barriers of fear and lies that we carry within us about other people. No doubt we are not actual mercenaries. But I know that I have carried fearful thinking about others in my heart, which has allowed me to form heartless opinions about them. And heartless opinions lead to heartless choices or thoughts. All life breathes together.

Grace

The grace of Understanding is so exquisite. This grace opens you to utilizing your inner gifts to assist others in articulating or examining an issue of the soul that seems out of reach to them. Forgiveness is a mystical experience, not an intellectual one. The mind cannot engage in an act of Forgiveness; only the soul can truly release. The mind craves vengeance and the hope that your aggressor will eventually acknowledge your pain. The ego is so tied up in this craving that it is nearly impossible for a person to forgive. Forgiveness simply does not make sense to a mind drowning in humiliation. It is a grace, the power of which compels us to act in a way that baffles our own mind at times. We may not even understand how we are able to forgive someone—only that we must.

Lord, let me receive the graces of Understanding and Forgiveness
—that I may be inspired by them from within,
and utilize them to help others.

38

THE WAY *of* THE TAO

Prayer

I HAVE TO ADMIT, LORD, that I sometimes wish You were more consistent—at least by my definition. I wish You would decide that I should navigate calm waters or a stormy sea and stick to the decision—rather than bringing me both in the same day. Then I could get the right gear on and not expect anything other than the sea I am sailing upon. Of course, I realize upon closer inspection what a foolish wish that is. After all, any captain sailing on calm seas for too long becomes careless, losing the fast, sharp, reactive survival instincts that made him an excellent captain in the first place. It is the storms that refine our instincts—not calm waters. We learn nothing napping in the sun. But likewise no captain can navigate through a storm forever without dying of exhaustion. I understand more and more that this chaos-to-calm design of life is one of perfection. It is *my* challenge to become an astute navigator. I am learning that my mind can be on a calm sea while my heart remains in a storm—or sometimes the other way around. If heaven is anything, it is consistent. It is the Tao. We are the navigators of our lives. Our exhaustion with the way of heaven comes from our expectations and endless insecurities, as I have learned time and again, Lord. We would like a certain wind—that celestial holy breeze—to take over for us so we can recognize the currents and the direction and our ETA. And perhaps most of all, we long to hear confirmation that heaven is controlling the flow of the wind. Then our fear-driven imagination no longer needs to torment us with "what might happen, somewhere in the future." Yet in the stillness of my soul, I always end up hearing or feeling or sensing that constant grace that tells me, "All is in order."

I cannot make up that sensation. And I will admit that at times I wish I could. I have wanted to run away from that voice and its majestic authority so many times—but where is there to run from You? It is that voice, that inner holy presence, I end up turning to even for the help I need to run away! The truth is, I must learn to navigate every storm as best I can. I must trust the way of both divine chaos and divine calm, for You, Lord, are the entire ocean.

Guidance

We cannot have light without darkness, or joy without sadness, or angels without demons. We cannot have only one side of life, no matter how much we wish it were so. We do not have the power to challenge the design of nature, though I have listened to people declare otherwise. They are the most frightened of all of us and generally have the most to lose in life. And so they cling to the illusion that they only have to *decide* that darkness does not exist—and thus it is so. What, then, should they tell the night? To just go away? We *need* the night. We need to withdraw into ourselves, into our unconscious—the unknown dimension of ourselves. We need our dreams and we need contact with the invisible realms. We are creatures of the celestial world temporarily visiting the mortal plane. We forget that truth only during daylight hours.

Grace

We are creatures governed by the law of Balance. The grace of Balance is inherent in that law. We can sense this grace coming into us when we explode in anger or stay for too long in that angry place. Or when we dwell in high states of imagination, without uniting our visions with grounded choices that activate the process of creation. Without the groundedness we remain "high" on ideas that go nowhere. The grace of Balance is unmistakable. Like a long, deep breath, it breaks through the grip of anger and fantasy-sized delusion. Like snapping you out of a spell you've been under, the grace of Balance returns you to your center point, as if to say, "Get a grip on yourself. Try again. Think clearly." How often after an encounter with this grace do we hear ourselves say, "What the heck was I thinking?"

Grant me the grace of Balance, Lord. Keep me in touch
with my inner nature so I can sense when I am out of Balance:
when I am swaying too far into my own familiar dark territory,
or on the other hand, too far into the light—which, since I know
not how to safely absorb so much power, may blind me.

39

HEALING *Night* FLIGHTS

Prayer

LORD, SEND YOUR HEALING angels to me tonight. Escort me out of my body and into the healing realm. Grant that they may repair my depleted soul, my weary body, and my burdened heart. May they clear the illusions from my mind and awaken me to what I need to see clearly about myself—my own actions, and all that I need to repair within myself. Let me rest in the silence of the celestial realm, calm in the company of angels as they heal what I am unable to heal due to my own limitations. Let their healing graces remain in my system and illuminate my thoughts with insight, my heart with love, and my body with stamina— that I might continue to serve on my path. Stand guard over me while I rest, and keep company with me while I sleep, protecting me from darkness. Let me remember in the depth of slumber that I am always watched over and in Your care. Shine Your grace of love and healing upon those I love and all humanity—the souls I share this journey of life with each day. I surrender my soul to this nocturnal journey, knowing that I will be returned to my body before the dawn.

Guidance

There is a healing realm of angels. Healing is their task, and it is a two-way enterprise. Heaven will not compensate for the work you must do on yourself. Heaven will not heal your darkness— that is up to you. If you ask for help to become a more integrous human being, the grace of integrity will be given. If you ask to become more generous of heart, the grace of generosity will be poured into you. If, however, you wake with the intention to remain selfish and to deceive others, don't imagine that you have experienced a great healing. For what in you has been healed? Heaven does not let us get away with anything—but it assists us with everything we ask. Teresa of Ávila wrote extensively that the path to the soul, and thus to God, was the path of self-knowledge: knowing who you are and what motivates you. You search out the dark until there is no more, and then you allow the light to speak to you. We fear the light because we think that a connection with the light will cost us our connection with our physical life. We have this fear—and dark belief—that in order to be physical, sexual, sensual, and in touch with pleasure, we need to be in league somehow with at least a touch of darkness. We need to avoid a clear rapport with our soul lest we be conscripted into a monastery. That is all nonsense—utter nonsense. The only time I ever experience people wanting any type of spiritual intervention is when they are desperately ill. Otherwise they want to keep God "at a distance" and their darkness mildly functional. They want to be able to hold on to "bite-sized" dark behaviors. But conscious dark behavior is not bite-sized. Someone is always harmed—be it yourself or someone you love—and committing conscious harm is the definition of what it means to sin. There is no such thing as a small act of darkness, just as there is no such thing as a small act of love.

Grace

The grace of Awakening is unfamiliar to people, though we often speak of it. Awakening is an experience just shy of having an epiphany—an explosion of the soul into the light. It is a sudden act of inner illumination in which you shift from not understanding the mystical meaning of a teaching or event into full realization. There is nothing small about a moment of Awakening. Therefore the grace of Awakening is a profound experience of personal illumination. You experience a deep insight about yourself that works as a spiritual depth charge, resulting in a permanent and very profound shift in how you comprehend your spiritual life.

Lord, grant me the grace to awaken—truly awaken— and the courage to embrace that mystical experience.

40

ORGANIC DIVINITY

Prayer

I DON'T RECALL EVER FEELING separated from the sacred thread within me—not really. I am not sure why. I have struggled with where I belong and what to do next, but it never occurred to me that You had dropped the ball on guiding me to that next stage of my life, Lord. It actually never occurred to me. I think I was born without ordinary appetites but with an extraordinary desire to find my way into the sacred realm, like a quest to find that secret garden. Perhaps that is why guidance was woven into my life. I have learned You have an organic voice. You guide us through the way of our own nature. I recall being mystified by my friends who knew they would be mothers even before they met their mates; motherhood was indeed a natural part of who they were. It was organic to them. I never had that organic pulse guiding me, so I watched motherhood from afar, never craving the need to give birth. I craved giving birth to books, to words on paper, incarnating the visions that electrified my imagination. Everyone craves their natural path, the way of their own nature. You are hidden along that path. Guidance abounds in that inner labyrinth. We crave to know what we are meant to give birth to in this life: what we are meant to create, to bring into fruition. Each of us, I deeply believe, longs to become fully whole with ourselves. I think that craving distraction—stuff, alcohol, drugs—is how we avoid encountering the power of our own nature. Which is ultimately You hidden in our blood and bones. There really is no way to avoid that encounter. One way or another, we are destined to meet.

Guidance

There is a reason why distractions never really satisfy us and why most distractions end up being harmful in some way. They get us into debt, they harm our health, or they throw our relationships off balance. We crave too much attention for our own good, or we eat too much, or we spend too much time on the computer—or the couch. Where we place our attention is a statement about how well we know what we really need and how clearly we understand that self-care includes others *because* it includes ourselves. At the end of the day, all roads lead to a single realization: that until you are living in your authentic skin, you will resent *not* living there. And you will find ways to punish either yourself or others, to express the anger created by your constant state of imbalance. That, too, is an expression of organic divinity—your spirit will not let you rest until you are conscious enough to recognize distractions. Only then can you choose not to engage with them.

Grace

Clarity is a grace that can strike us like a bolt of lightning. Just like that, our understanding of something shifts, as if a sparkle of light were lit, illuminating a thought we had never before considered. In that instant, we experience a Clarity that penetrates through every cell tissue in our being. That is the power of this grace.

Grant me the grace of Clarity, Lord. Especially in moments when I cannot see my way through difficulties or when I feel lost in the confusion of my own thoughts. And most of all, help me act on the direction of that grace.

41

THE CURIOUS MATTER *of* MEANING *and* PURPOSE

Prayer

WHAT IN MY LIFE DOES *not* have meaning and purpose? I am the one who brings meaning to everything I do or see. I give purpose to all my tasks. Nothing has meaning or purpose on its own. I am the one who decides that for me, gardening is the exquisite act of spending time with nature, sharing the intimate experience of planting seeds, and participating in the cycle of life. I am not on my knees digging dirt. I gratefully plunge my hands into the soil, amazed and in awe that once again, in return for my planting flowers and vegetables in this dark, fertile ground, the Earth will nurture these small, sturdy plants and my garden will yet again bloom into a living bouquet of astonishing splendor. Nothing is as meaningful to me as nurturing life, in any form. If purpose cannot be experienced through that, Lord, then what? Nurturing others through passing on knowledge or giving time or caring for the Earth is meaningful. I have never once felt that being present to and for another person was a meaningless thing to do. Knowing that I am the one who gives meaning and purpose to my life is like discovering the secret of life itself.

Guidance

I cannot even count the number of people I have met who are on a quest for meaning and purpose yet have no idea where to look or even what they are seeking. What exactly do "meaning and purpose" look like? They wonder if such a discovery will require moving residences or an investment of capital. Why do we find the truth so disquieting—that *we* are the engines of all that has meaning and purpose in our lives? We decide, by choice, that we will do a task with all our hearts—or not. The act of doing what is asked of you, or what is demanded of you by necessity, with an open heart is actually a living prayer. It is a way of saying to the heavens that nothing asked of you is insignificant, that even if the task at hand does not suit your vanity, you do not consider its placement in your world to be a divine error. Your entire life becomes *a mystery filled with meaningfulness*—instead of an endless search for purpose.

Grace

The grace of Wonder is like receiving a blast of bliss. Instead of worrying because something seems out of place or unfair, the sensation of Wonder lifts you into the experience of awe. How can anything be as perfect as a rose in full bloom? Stars cease to be stars and for an instant become diamonds glittering in the night sky, suddenly revealing a glimpse of the extraordinary beauty of the cosmos. Until the grace of Wonder opened your eyes, the night sky was just the night sky. But after seeing it through grace, the cosmos speaks to you. And somehow you know you are a part of this magnificent, alive Universe.

Everything has meaning, and everyone has purpose. I cannot see the invisible threads of creation connecting all that I do. So I bless all that I do and dwell in the grace of Wonder that I am connected to the whole fabric of life—and that this fabric is connected back to me.

42

THE POWER *of* CO-CREATION

Prayer

WHAT IS IT THAT I AM CREATING with this soul of mine? I need to become ever more aware of the power it contains. Every flash of love or fear or joy or anger generates a creative consequence. I now observe the response a smile sparks when I walk past a stranger. Just like that, the atmosphere around us on the street shifts as the silent message is communicated that I am not a threat. A smile returned tells me, "And neither am I." And the street suddenly seems to me like it is electric with grace. Our two smiles have suddenly transformed the atmosphere—just like that. What a wonder we are, Lord. I am truly in awe of how the soul works with the mystical laws. Karma tells us that what goes around comes around. Jesus said we reap what we sow. The Buddha spoke of the wheel of *samsara*. I think it is wise to assume we are accountable for our choices—because what else makes sense? We are wired to remember our choices, to feel them, to hang on to those we regret through guilt. We would not be creatures of learning in this way if we were not meant to learn from our mistakes. I imagine that when I depart this Earth, all that I have worried about and everything that seems so significant right now will evaporate. I will realize how insignificant all these stresses and worries really are. By the time I disincarnate, the time for responding will have passed. The thought of that moment is an outrageous blessing of perspective, Lord. I cannot afford to waste the precious gift of my life on petty nonsense. I will not carry darkness about others or life in my heart. I do not want that energy to inspire the choices I make. In the time I have left, I want to become more and more outrageous. Each year I want to hear Your voice within me ever more clearly. If this life is about co-creation, then let's give it all we've got. If something goes bad, Lord—I'll just blame You. Kidding . . .

Guidance

When I was 20 years old I had a dream in which I was taken 20 years into my future, to age 40. The dream was prompted, I suspect, by my not getting an editorial position I had set my sights on. I was devastated and had decided—at 20 years old—that I was destined for failure. In the dream I became aware that I was "40," and I was instructed to recall what was so troubling to me "back" when I was 20. I said I couldn't recall at all. Then I heard a sort of laugh, and I was told to remember upon waking that I could not recall what the trouble was—and I did remember. I have relived that dream more times than I can count throughout the years, having passed by age 40 some time ago. It has served me as a guide all my life. When something is upsetting me, I will project forward and ask myself, "Will I even remember this a year from now? Two years from now?" And with that, I am able to react in the present. (I am eventually going to run out of years to project ahead—ha!) I offer this lesson to you as the holy grace of wisdom it was to me so long ago.

Grace

Wisdom lasts a lifetime. One drop of Wisdom goes the distance of your life. Wisdom is one of the graces you can seek out. Read books on Wisdom, absorb it, dwell in it, reflect upon it. Allow the wise guidance of the ancestors—who were inspired by angels—to inspire you.

Let me embrace Wisdom in whatever way it comes to me
—whether through the words of an elder or the needs
of a child or the feedback of a friend.

43

FEAR IN *the* ATMOSPHERE

Prayer

I CAN SENSE SO MUCH FEAR in the atmosphere, Lord. All life breathes together. How can we not sense each other if we sit still long enough and listen through the portals of our soul? All life changes constantly and together. Nothing could be more obvious to me now. Extraordinary, unfamiliar changes are now penetrating into our blood and bones, into our psyches and our souls. I know we have crossed a Rubicon greater than anything in the history of humanity, Lord. What a moment this is to be alive. And we are newcomers in this energetic territory. The Earth is not new. We are morphing into a new type of human being, one that can see and perceive, hear and sense. I think, Lord, that we are awakening to the age of the soul. I have no doubt at all that this will be a very different world once human beings realize the power of our souls. I wonder at times how rapidly a person would heal if she could call upon the healing power of the human inner-net, the prayers of millions, indeed billions, directed toward one soul. Or toward one cause, ending a conflict. We are the engines that generate the events we experience. People speak of co-creating their realities all the time, Lord. If only they really understood and lived the power of that mystical truth. We truly are all one.

Guidance

Every breath you take contains the breath of every person on the planet. That is a mystical truth, not a literal one. Yet the oxygen we breathe is filled with particles of life from all over the place, air that has hovered over every continent on this planet. We eat food from other countries, grown from soil mixed with the compost of the local population. Nature is amazing as she recycles . . . well, us, along with the rest of nature. Is it any wonder that we also recycle the emotional debris of our fellow human beings through our energy systems? And we do. I have shared this mystical truth many times with students, observing how many respond to that revelation with utter panic. "What should I do? How do I cleanse myself of that?" I have to laugh. Do you think a few organic vegetables will somehow separate you from the fundamental design of life—that all is one? My suggestion, as I have said to so many, is that when you feel anxiety and stress building up in your energy system, do not assume that it is necessarily yours. You may be channeling collective anxiety and stress, breathing collective psychic free radicals generated by all of us. Grace, generated through prayer, is the antidote.

Grace

The grace of healing Love is the remedy for collective stress and anxiety. Healing Love is also the most effective grace for your personal stress. Stress is a very modern word, one that is a catchall for irritations of all kinds—from the inability to react with anger when we want to, to not being able to take control of a situation, to not having everything our way all the time. When the balance of power in your life is no longer in your favor, you feel stress and anxiety. The darkness of your own inner narrative—as well as the shared collective narrative that things are out of control—suggests that harm is coming. Our personal fear feeds that collective narrative and in turn, fear comes back to us even more strongly. Healing Love has a near miraculous way of releasing you from this loop. Healing Love can break the current of negative energy and rekindle embers of love for people you were convinced you could never again like, much less love. Healing Love is a grace that wipes the slate clean of past wounds. This is something our mind cannot do, as we count on our mind to provide strategies for self-protection. Healing Love has only one strategy: to let love do the healing.

---

*Lord, let me be a channel for healing Love, through me
and around me. At the slightest indication of anxiety, let this grace
flood into me, drowning the fears that rise up like reptiles inside me.
All life breathes together, and therefore, Lord, all life heals together.*

44

SURRENDERING CONTROL

Prayer

LORD, HELP ME STAY consciously in grace. Every moment of my life, I am participating in an act of creation. Every thought, every feeling, every sensation generates a consequence—a next thought, an emotion, a choice. The realization that I am a living, breathing creature of unlimited creative power is so great a truth that I am awestruck by it. No wonder there is karma—we are bound to our choices forever, for where do action and reaction end? I am not conscious enough to manage the power of my soul by myself; that much I have concluded. For all the quiet encounters I have had with the holy realm, and even knowing what little I do about how heaven works, I am still often angry and judgmental at what goes on in this world. It is a chaotic place, and fear erupts endlessly. And as You know, I contribute to that cesspool of anger constantly. My temper is my curse. It is difficult to live in the truth that everything is an illusion. I am not a conscious or enlightened human being. I am a novice on the spiritual path. I often do not think about the consequences of my actions and my thoughts as often as I should. So, I ask that You stand between me and all those whom I might unknowingly hurt with my thoughts and actions. Let the angels act as a fire wall against my negative thoughts and fears so that others are not harmed by the fears within me that I have yet to conquer. I open myself to Your guidance and release my need to have expectations of the day and of others. In *surrendering* my need for control, I entrust my life to You. Hover over me, Lord. I am new at trusting You fully. I will probably slip up, but I know what the path looks like now. Keep the light bright. I will always find my way back.

Guidance

We cannot acknowledge our participation in the creation of our realities without considering *how* that is so. Through what means do we do co-create? Human beings have always had choice. Yet something sets us apart from previous generations who would never have imagined they were participants in creating their life experiences, health, relationships, and creative opportunities. So what is it that we are discovering about ourselves? We are realizing the authority and power of our soul. We are now in the era of organic divinity. Whether it's health, joy, suffering, inspiration, or coping with loss, the search for how and why things happen as they do will lead you to the same place: the vast domain behind your eyes. You will discover that somehow you had a hand in creating all that unfolded, and continues to unfold, in your life. Your soul is your power source. Whether your participation was obvious or subtle, you have never been energetically disconnected from anything that has happened in your life. Becoming conscious of our choices does not spare us from the cycles of life, incidentally. We will never avoid death or aging or illness or loss. Life is life, after all. But in this new world, self-inflicted suffering is becoming optional.

Grace

The grace of Trust is woven into the act of surrender. You Trust that the grace of heaven is at work in every moment of your life. Whether pain or pleasure, loss or gain, win or lose—what unfolds in this moment is no way to evaluate the whole of the journey you are on. One bad meal is no way to judge all the food in Italy. You have no idea what's being prepared for you at all the other restaurants you have yet to visit. Surrender requires detachment and the wisdom to act on guidance as given to you. Everyone knows what that feels like when they are being guided not to eat something, for example. That guidance is as real and divine as a visionary dream. No matter in what form guidance comes to you, when it does, act on it. Surrender to it. Heaven never speaks in paragraphs, and it never sends unnecessary messages.

Grant me the grace of Trust, Lord, now and always. I hardly Trust myself, so trusting You will be a work in progress. One thing I do know is that getting to that place of Trust will make my life much easier.

45

ONE *with* ALL BEINGS

Prayer

I HAVE TO ADMIT SOMETHING today, Lord. I am having an attack of arrogance. Not a big attack . . . just a flashback of my old self. I heard a scientist talk about how the Universe—this entire endless vast space of creation—all started from a bang. Did it? Really? Wow . . . I think that's absolute nonsense. (See what I mean about the arrogance?) Not until I hear a scientist speak of the other dimensions of consciousness and the many sacred realms of creation can any of them speak about how all of this began. I decided better You tell him than me. All I know is that all life is holy, and I am so grateful, so very grateful to know that. I marvel at this whole theater of creation—the stars, the galaxies, the vastness of all the eye can see. I am in awe of how every living being on the Earth goes about its day, doing its task. Birds take to the skies, and aquatic creatures commune underwater, hidden from the human eye. Life is everywhere, always giving birth and always returning to the Earth. And the Earth keeps us all alive. Every living creature sharing this planet is sustained through the graciousness of this magnificent being of life, planet Earth. Lord, break open my heart enough that all living creatures can find a loving place to rest in grace within me. Let me pray for them each day. Keep me ever mindful that I am here for such a short time that I must do what I can to nurture this Earth, to care for and about life in whatever ways I can. I admit that I have been slow to offer my help in the past. I have looked the other way, preferring to believe that I am safe in my comfortable world. I will keep my eyes open now.

Guidance

As much as we crave our individuality and our own space, we are paradoxically unable to separate ourselves from the whole fabric of life. We are by design creatures of wholeness, of oneness. We actually *belong to each other.* That is a mystical truth. And if we lived by that truth, imagine how well we would take care of each other. It's a truth worth dwelling in for a while.

Grace

Feeling nurtured is like being in contact with life force. People will travel a long distance to return to a person or a place for Nurturing. Imagine that warm sensation elevated to the power of grace. It's not unlike shifting from a lovely cologne to its perfect perfume essence. As a grace, Nurturing is expressed in its pure strength. When it flows through your soul, this grace compels you to care for others, even for those with whom you have no personal connection. Your heart opens, and you feel the need to respond. Simple as that.

I know how wonderful it feels to be nurtured, Lord.
Open my heart to the grace of Nurturing, that I may
serve others in ways that I have been served.

46

THE GIFT *of* AGING

Prayer

I MUST SAY, LORD, ONE THING about aging that has surprised me—and it really has—is that I feel more outrageously loving the older I get. Between You and me, I am curious about that. I've noticed that the older I've gotten, the less I want of anything. What I *do* want now is to know more about life, to understand more about people, and to do more for others. And here's the thing about love—whatever love is: I find it so easy to see the good in people without having to look so hard for it. Not that it was all that difficult before, but let's just say it took more time. Lord, I have to say I am grateful to You for the gift of aging. It *is* a gift. With each passing year, I appreciate my life more, and everyone in it. My gratitude often brings tears to my eyes as I realize except for the grace of You, all might be different. And indeed, all might well be different someday. I don't know what tomorrow may bring. I cannot help but notice how many times I have left a restaurant having filled myself with delicious food and within minutes, I pass a hungry, homeless person. I notice that more now. I can no longer just walk past that person as if he does not matter. I have to feed that person. Why else did I see him? We must share what we have been given. We have no business expecting to be looked after by You if we do not, in turn, look after others. I've discovered that aging makes this so much easier because *giving* takes over *craving*. That's freedom. And oh, how I love my freedom. I think I shall be a wilder woman the older I get. I suggest You make loving and caring for others the cure for Alzheimer's. Just a thought.

Guidance

One of the more foolish things I have noticed about people these days is their odd relationship with aging. We put so much effort into staying healthy so we can force this physical body of ours to stay in shape, look young, stay vital, and so on—and yet we cannot handle admitting our age as the years go by. Instead of celebrating the very goals we are working so hard to accomplish, we lament the passing of the years. We hope that the latter years of our lives won't be lonely, useless, or who knows what else. What is wrong with our thinking? Every year is the beginning of a new storyline, a new adventure—and more freedom. Free yourself from the burden of wanting things, of needing to accomplish anything, of being driven by the desire to please others. Finally close your eyes and listen to the wild voice of your soul and let go.

Grace

Courage is a grace with so many expressions. The soul is a wild and free inner companion, full of endless inspiration and holy mischief. But it sometimes takes Courage to get into holy mischief. We have all read the stories and poems written by people during the last months and even days of their lives. They read like wish lists of what could have been—had they only mustered the Courage to liberate themselves from the constraints that held power over them in their younger, healthier days. Have the Courage to be a holy mischief maker. Put your whole heart and soul into it. As you prepare to leave this life, and your thoughts inevitably turn to what you *could* have done, may you not wish that you had been more courageous.

Lord, the idea of becoming a holy mischief maker has never occurred to me—but why not? I like the sound of it. So, grant me the Courage to step out of my comfort zone and into the realm of playful imagination. I usually ask for Your help in times of need. But in truth, I need to lighten up, to play more, to be more at ease with this business of life. We only associate You with problems, Lord. No one thinks of You as a playmate. You should work on that. Kidding!

47

WHAT IS *the* SPIRITUAL PATH?

Prayer

HOW DO I DESCRIBE THE spiritual path to another, Lord? Help me out. I am asked about the spiritual path so often. It is not a small question. Yet every time I answer it for someone, which is all the time, I listen to myself making something up. Should I tell that person the truth? Should I tell people that my spiritual path amounts to quiet times of contemplation with You? I ponder, I ask, I listen, I wait, I wait, I wait . . . and then when I am distracted, busy with my day, thoughts occur to me that have nothing to do with what I am thinking at the time. But they are always the answers to the questions I was praying about earlier that day or the day before— sometimes much longer ago than that. I always know the answer to a prayer will arrive. The timing is up to You. I ask; You answer. Silence is also an answer. That truth took me a while to adjust to, but I have learned to trust it. I have also learned that I must ask with detachment and receive without expectation. It took me years and years and years to grasp that dynamic. How simple it would be to just tell each person that their entire life is their spiritual path. Every relationship we have is a companion on our spiritual path, like it or not. Now, do with your life what you want. I asked one person what exactly it was he was seeking on his path. He said he wasn't sure. But I was: he was looking for romantic love. Love, not You. But falling in love is also a part of the spiritual path—he'll find that out. How simple this business of the spiritual quest would be if only people really understood that everything is a manifestation of the partnership between the human spirit and the Divine.

Guidance

This business of separating your ordinary life from your spiritual path is a holdover from traditional religious teachings: the separation of church and state, body and soul, and heaven and Earth. The age of separation—the age of Pisces—is coming to an end. We are rapidly being absorbed into the era of wholism. Spiritually, archetypally, scientifically, medically, technically, and globally. We are now able to understand this mystical truth: that there is no separation between the energetics of life and the physical realm. Matter and energy are intimately interconnected. Energy is the fuel, the life force of matter. Applying that mystical law to the spiritual path translates thus: Everything, and everyone, in your life is a vital part of your spiritual path. You, in turn, are a part of theirs. This realization may inspire you to live more consciously, more ethically, more generously—or not. But one thing is for certain: your biology responds to the spiritual truth that is active in your soul. That means that the sources of biological stress for us have markedly increased. A generation ago, stress was generated through overwork or adultery or financial concerns. Today we must cope with stress generated by *not living in alignment with what we know to be truth*. Many people do not recognize that the source of their anxiety and depression runs far deeper than ordinary conflict. Their stress is soul deep, originating in the fact that they are consciously compromising sacred truths. That is a crisis of the soul, and the soul communicates directly to the mind and the body. The soul thrives on truth. It will become a relentless inner opponent if you violate those truths. That, in a nutshell, is how the spiritual path relates to the grit of everyday life.

Grace

The grace of Endurance is often required to cope with ourselves. Sometimes the most challenging obstacle we have to deal with is our own nature, including our contradictory behavior, our weaknesses, and the dilemmas they lead to. We would like to blame others for our faults. But at the end of the day, we are the only inhabitants of our body. We are the only ones making our choices. We are far too old to blame our parents for our adult behavior. The grace of Endurance brings a big sigh. It fills us with the sense of relaxation and the knowledge that we will "get through" the difficulty we are in. Endurance communicates that there are challenges in life that we simply must, well, endure. And yet, at the same time, that all troubles eventually and inevitably pass.

Grant me the grace of Endurance, Lord. I need this grace, this extra light, to get through my own distractions and to endure the upheaval that comes along with embracing truth.

48

REJECTION IS PROTECTION

Prayer

I SAW SUCH SORROW ON A friend's face today, Lord. Something did not work out the way she had hoped. There was once a time when I would have prayed for her to get the position she was aiming for. When I think of that now, how I used to pray, I wince in my soul. It took me years—and maybe lifetimes—to understand my folly. Thinking that I know what is best for someone, and that You require my guidance—my intervention—to direct the future of another person's life! I often replay the dream I had years ago, at the time I felt the doors had suddenly closed on the career I had chosen. I had been lamenting not getting my way. I was feeling sorry for myself, rejected by something I wanted, and abandoned by heaven, so to speak. I was not in good shape. But in a dream visitation I was informed that "earthly rejection is holy protection." I woke up calm. Tranquil, as if I had slept under a blanket of grace. I have never doubted again—not once. When I released my unmet expectations to You, You led me down a path I did not see coming. One I could not have imagined because I never knew it existed. I never knew I was a medical intuitive until it was the only door left open. I will never forget that August afternoon when I got the mystical message that I had to leave Chicago and go—immediately—to New Hampshire. You let me know I had to do it or I would be "called home." Not a threat, just a fact. I wasn't the least bit afraid. I heard You, as if I were receiving my next instructions. I have always followed those instructions. If it were not for my blind trust in You, Lord, I would never have moved or been able to endure the isolation that followed. It was in the midst of that lonely, rural New Hampshire silence that my calling emerged. Clever, You. I did not even realize that classic mystical setup until years later. That's how prayers are answered: some doors get locked and others get opened. And then there's the waiting room. I know my friend is now in that waiting room, fearing that no door will open for her again now that this one has shut. I know better, though I have no idea what You're up to. I told her to just surrender the mess of everything to You. Earthly chaos is really your sandbox. You will reroute her life. I told her not to interfere with Your plans for her. No offering You advice or limitations or restrictions. Surrender means surrender. Let go, and let You have at it.

Guidance

The spiritual plan for your life is an ongoing plan. It doesn't start and stop, like jobs you begin and quit. Our blind spot—and it is a big one—is our insistence that God become a business partner. That divine guidance present as something practical, efficient, and financially useful. Guidance works from within us as well as around us, to be sure. Heaven does express itself through events such as locked and open doors. But these external events are not ends in and of themselves; they are here to serve our *internal* spiritual life. Heaven does not solve our problems for us; it inspires us with resolutions, ways to initiate action in the world, for the purpose of furthering our soul's journey. The Divine cannot make choices for us, but it can—and does—set up blockades for our own protection. Every movement in your life has purpose. It does not matter that we do not see the purpose in the moment or the plan or the timing of when and how the next step will unfold. Well, it matters to us, of course, in practical ways, but if you could let go of the practical and trust the miraculous, the hidden ways of the Divine at work behind the scenes in your life, you would realize that nothing is ever as it seems.

Grace

We need the grace of Trust more than we realize. We want everything to happen now—right now—in our lives. And we want to recognize the sound of every footstep we hear. We have to stop wanting, wanting, wanting life to be what it will never, ever be— familiar, controllable, and wrapped around our personal needs. That impossible craving is what leads to attacks of stress, panic, and inner madness. Instead we must contact the grace of Trust. We must learn to rest easy in the mobius of prayer and trust, guidance and action. Rather than imagining greatness or humiliation, power or powerlessness. Your imagination is an engine of creation, a vessel through which your *inside* coordinates the *outside* of your life. Imagining greatness for yourself is rooted in the fear of humiliation. The end product is an ego full of hubris. Driven by fear, you will end up in the fog of panic and uncertainty. The discipline—and it *is* a discipline—is to apply the grace of Trust. Trust brings detachment. You do not have to interfere with heaven's work. If you knew what was best for you, you would not need heaven's help. Just Trust.

Lord, bless me with the grace of Trust. I will no doubt have to say this prayer again and again. I wish I were as good at trusting as I am at doubting, but isn't that what grace is about? You can Trust me to pray—that is my part. And I will Trust that this grace is present within, and that heaven is hidden behind every closed door.

49

WHERE IS GOD?

Prayer

LORD, YOU KNOW THAT DISASTERS, catastrophes, epidemics, wars, and the slaughter of innocents make people question the existence of God. They feel as if You do not exist, or at the very least You've been AWOL. I can't say I blame them. How is a person supposed to make sense out of horror on a massive scale, especially when it's man-made? We speak of You—"Why does God behave like this?"—as if You were a human being expected to follow rules of human behavior. That would work for us because then we could second-guess You, bribe You, outwit You, see You coming in the dark. We could continue to tell ourselves that bad things only happened to bad people—and furthermore, *we* are the *good* people. You would always be on *our* side, protecting our property and family. Rarely, Lord, do I meet someone at a workshop who wants help to heal their own vengeful thoughts or their heart full of wrath. Instead, so many people share that they are still, after so many years, seeking answers about how someone could have hurt them so much. I sometimes want to shake them like a rag doll—I will admit that. And I know that is a weakness in me. But I also see it as a strength. I see no point in indulging in the meaningless quest for why a damaged parent did not love a child. What is it people are really looking for? They want to scream that they are hurt, and they want that pain to hurt their parent. And it never, ever works. Mostly, they end up disappointed. But a part of this quest is anger at You—whether consciously or unconsciously. They are angry at the hand they have been dealt in their lives. They want an explanation. They want You to make all things better, to somehow make the rest of their lives easier. They want their suffering rewarded, like chips earned at the pain game. I don't support this view: that somehow You screwed up because they had a difficult childhood. Injustice is hard, Lord. That, in a nutshell, sums up the last days of Jesus. Injustice is so difficult because we want to control the order of life and everyone in it. But cruelty and destruction are caused by that very craving, the madness for control. If people truly understood the ongoing presence and power of divine order unfolding in every moment, we would no longer feel we had to control nature. We would only have to participate in its cycles. The loss of life brought on by eruptive events would be understood as organic losses, not a product of good or evil. They would not be viewed as crimes and punishments, new reasons to question whether You exist. I have to say, I am so bored with the question of your existence, Lord. I have to keep myself from rolling my eyes when I hear it. I have to keep myself from asking, "What? You, too?" But I don't. Well . . . maybe when I get home.

Guidance

We are governed by the laws of nature, both mystical and physical. They mirror each other. The mystical laws initiate acts of creation and the physical laws manage them. It's not complicated. Choices generate consequences. Collective negative choices generate vast resources of what I think of as psychic free radicals. This, too, is logic—the physics of creation. Likewise, prayer generates grace. Vast resources of grace channel inspiration to individuals and groups, supporting courage, benevolence, and acts of service. Human beings do not have to suffer from wars or local conflicts or terrorist attacks. These are *optional* nightmares, choices we make. When we ask, "How could this terrible event happen? Where was God?" the answer is "Hidden in the power of nature: human nature, Mother Nature, and Divine Nature." That is the cosmic holy trinity.

Grace

Humility is one of the graces that spiritual masters most emphasized. The grace of Humility is like getting coated with a nonstick spray that detaches you from the power hunger that is so destructive in our lives. Arrogance and pride are the source of so much suffering, which could be avoided if a person had the protection of this one grace.

Lord, protect me with the grace of Humility. Protect me from my own worst instincts, from actions driven by pride and fear. Help me stay focused on the truth that only You have the power to direct my life unless I release that power to others out of fear and anger.

50

THE DEMON'S VOICE

Prayer

THE REALITY OF THE DARK underbelly of life is getting exposed, Lord. The modern mind has decided to rewrite the order of creation, dismissing the night but keeping the day. Tossing out the shadow but retaining the services of the sun. Clever how darkness works! We've shifted our vocabulary to anesthetize the words that describe evil so we can no longer see or recognize its influence. We cannot recognize its handiwork if we don't have the words to describe it. The word *conscience* has been retired. It's been replaced by the rather vacant term *consciousness*. A word so vague it can mean whatever a person wants it to mean. The fear of the dark has gone primal, Lord. I can see the immediate discomfort that arises in people at the mention of "the Devil." They make sarcastic wisecracks to calm their nerves—or walk out of the room. Or they openly comment that they do not believe in evil, much less the Devil. But their discomfort tells me otherwise. They are running from the truth, not from me. I imagine some people think I am having a flashback to medieval Catholicism when I bring it up. Yet all of those reactions tell me how frightened of darkness they are and how vulnerable they have become to its influence. I check them out for trinkets, crystals, good luck charms—dangling tokens of protection from negativity. All indicators to me of their fragility. The word "negativity" has been substituted for "the Devil" because that word lacks an obvious connection to the myths of hell. It is a neutral word, bypassing the sacred completely. We've gotten very good at word games, Lord. Teresa of Ávila always told her nuns that the moment you believe you are safe from darkness, it is standing right next to you. I know that all too well, Lord. Like everyone else, I thought I was immune to encounters with evil. Like a spoiled child, I assumed that I was protected from it. Then I was robbed. And it brought home the truth that anything can happen to me—theft, rape, murder. That experience began my inner excavation into what I believed I deserved. From You, from life—from who knows what. I emerged from the inner quest realizing that there is no order to the Universe that spins around me. In spite of my faith and trust. The order of life, of nature, is greater than *my* life. Who was I to think I should be immune to all the darkness in the world? Teresa of Ávila prayed *Lead me not into temptation* constantly, knowing that pride was her adversary. She knew the dark whispers of evil—the reptiles in her soul—could penetrate her through her pride. They softly reminded her of her worst fear: that she could indeed be put on trial as a heretic, found guilty, and burned at the stake. Just as angels inspire us with grace-filled thoughts and often surround us with calmness and courage, demons know our weaknesses and animate them with fear. You've made this world an equal playing field. That's for sure.

Guidance

No one really wants to believe in the presence of darkness or its influence. We don't want it to be true that demons are "roaming the Earth." But they are. You have no difficulty imagining angels. I suspect you have called upon "your" personal angel and felt like you have received help. (If I hear another comment about a parking angel, I'll scream.) But what about "your" demon? Why does that seem so implausible? It's the child in you that can imagine an angel, but oh no, not a "bad guy." Well, that's not the design of the universe. There are good cops *and* bad cops. That is the nature of polarity. We have the shadow *and* the light within us. Spiritual teachers since forever have taught their students to pray for guidance and protection—Jesus among them. It wasn't because these holy teachers lacked a modern-day education. It was because they knew the landscape of the invisible world. And they understood the power of one human soul, not to mention the collective power of humanity. If darkness were not powerful, why would we struggle so much to find the light?

Grace

Discernment is considered one of the highest graces. It is the soul's aptitude to pierce through the illusions that diminish our inherent strength, clarity, compassion, and sense of moral justice. Illusions are easily created. We decide to take a comment personally that had nothing to do with us, or we conclude that we could handle a drink—just one drink—because we've been sober for two years and this is such a special occasion . . . Oh, how we know that voice! That part of ourselves that gives us permission to do all things harmful, weak, deceptive, and even nasty. We *count on* that voice to provide us with an excuse for bad behavior. This is where holding on to wounds is useful. The old "I'm weak because of my childhood" excuse. But the truth is, one day we each have to confront our partnership with darkness. We have to acknowledge that the partnership is a *conscious* one. We have to become discerning about our own actions, not remain helpless victims of our own emotions. We are not all that helpless. We just like playing in the dark . . .

Lord, I need the grace of Discernment to see my
inner self clearly. I need to discern when I am courting
darkness, when I am listening to it, and when I am consciously
giving in to it. I already know when I am lying or breaking my word.
But I have not openly admitted that breaking my word or lying are
acts of darkness. They are, Lord. And I have to acknowledge my own
conscious dark behaviors, more than those of others. Now I need the
grace to discern why I dance with that darkness, why I allow myself
to partner with the dark, and I need to break that connection.
God, grant me this grace. This is not going to be easy.

51

THE QUIET *of* DEVOTION

Prayer

OVERCAST DAYS WARM MY SOUL and make me think of poetry and contemplation and all things cozy. I automatically withdraw into inner dialogues by habit—and desire. My thoughts turn upward and inward these days, Lord. I listen with my cell tissue now for those subtle light currents that pour down from heaven. Some are filled with guidance and others with the grace of calm and tranquility. I delight in these moments. They recharge my soul. I can sense life beyond this life swirling around me, like a brief visitation. Funny how these moments make worries evaporate. Nothing seems impossible or even that difficult. Problems become just what they are—temporary obstacles that will fade in time. The less we respond to them, the faster they evaporate. Suffering, Lord, is a matter that does not so easily evaporate. Being contained in a body that is at war with disease is not a simple matter. Neither is grief. Yet these earthly burdens—which feel like titanium barriers to us—are penetrated easily by prayer. I sometimes think these obstacles give You an opportunity to reveal how clever You can be at answering prayers. Perhaps the resolution to human suffering is also found in the truth that everyone shares these experiences in one way or the other. They are part of the fabric of life and we are part of that weave. We will all grieve at some point, we will all mourn the passing of loved ones, and we will all know illness—one day, our own. But that truth does not diminish the greater truth of the ever-present companionship of heaven each day. No matter what that day brings, from birth to death. We are escorted into life and we are escorted back to heaven. In between, we listen . . . we listen . . . we listen.

Guidance

So many people have asked me how to pray—where to begin and what to listen for when they pray. Holy listening is simple. It's just *listening*. But being quiet is not the same as holy listening. The latter includes observation—with your body and your being. Stop wanting anything. Cease anticipating a reward for praying. Above all else, relinquish the craving to hear cogent guidance—as if you were listening for instructions from a human being. God is not a human being. Mystical guidance enters into you softly, like a thought that suddenly occurs to you out of the blue. I have learned to take notice of that "sudden, out of nowhere" sensation. Mystical guidance is well timed and well placed, so as not to be missed. Holy listening is the practice of waiting and waiting and waiting—and while waiting, consciously releasing your inner debris and nocturnal reptiles. That's the clutter in your mind, the chaos you listen to that prevents you from entering into stillness. People often think tranquility and inner peace are somehow found "out there" somewhere. But every worthy state of consciousness—from love to compassion to discernment and all the other graces—is discovered within.

Grace

Holy listening requires the grace of Devotion. Showing up for prayer, even the five minutes you commit to holy listening, should be considered a spiritual devotion. It's more than a practice; it's an inner vow. Your soul vows to show up. We require grace to keep such vows. At times the grace of Devotion can feel like a ball and chain, attaching us to our commitment. It reminds us—through guilt if necessary—that we are neglecting our spiritual commitment. There is nothing easy about this grace. This grace can also express itself through revealing to us deeper reasons for why we were inspired to make this particular commitment to, for example, holy listening for five minutes a day.

Grant me the grace of Devotion, especially when my tendency to sabotage my spiritual practice arises—as I know it will. I need to break through that barrier, that wall that prevents me from reaching the interior of my soul. Grant me this grace, Lord, even though it is often difficult to carry.

52

THE MYSTERY *of* YOU

Prayer

I WAS ASKED YET AGAIN how You work, and whether praying really does any good. I have to tell You that sometimes I wish You would show up and answer these questions for Yourself. It's exasperating. I have so much proof—and simultaneously, no way to prove it. How do I explain how You work when I hardly understand it myself? Who can possibly explain divine intervention? And yet I have had so many experiences of mystical encounters with heaven. What do I tell others? These encounters are between You and me—and that is the mystery of it all. You never leave any obvious evidence in Your wake, only the type that requires faith. I realized quite some time ago that words are useless when it comes to explaining You. Perhaps you should part the ocean again, pull another Moses routine. But even if you did, I know how human beings would respond: we would find a scientific reason for why it happened. You would fade into the background yet again. Science and You—not good bedfellows. And yet, the physicists are now floating around in mystical territory, studying light and energy. I imagine they'll run into You soon enough, likely through an anomaly that defies their calculations. But not Yours. For You reside within anomalies, always hiding in the unexplainable. So, what should I tell people when they ask if praying to You does any good? I have asked some people to tell me why they are asking that question in the first place. I already know the answer, but it is they who need to admit it. They have progressed beyond mere "problems" and are now dealing with the type of suffering that cannot be healed through ordinary options. Finally, they must consider whether divine Intervention is really possible. I often tell people that they have nothing to lose by praying to You. Praying never harmed anyone, I tell them. But deep down, I know without a doubt that You will respond with an outpouring of grace. You will flood them with holy light from the celestial realm . . . would that they could only see it. Even science would find it difficult to explain such light, piercing through the sky like a laser. All it takes to open this floodgate is one prayer.

Guidance

It seems people cannot stop wondering about how prayer works. This is especially true at our most desperate moments. Perhaps you are experiencing such a moment in your life right now. There is nothing more ordinary than wanting immediate resolution to a crisis—our own or that of a loved one. Fear and worry are brutal to bear, especially where matters of survival are concerned. We become desperate to know how we will get through a financial crisis or an illness or a legal matter. Understand this: Prayer influences actions that are in the process of unfolding. Heaven works behind the scenes. And yet . . . every other person's life is woven into the events of our own. Our needs—and therefore our prayers—must blend somehow into the greater good of the whole. No situation is just about us. Prayers are always answered, and in a way that serves all concerned.

Grace

The grace of Generosity has so many expressions. They go well beyond the obvious, such as giving to the poor or sharing bread at the table. That is the basic expression of what it means to be generous. As an expression of grace, however, Generosity blows open the doors of your heart, making it possible for you to recognize and even pray for the needs of others. You find it's possible to wish your adversaries to be as looked after by heaven as you would have heaven look after you. Such a generous prayer is an acknowledgement that you see the whole picture, that life is not a dynamic of right and wrong but an unfolding of events and relationships. An endless balancing of karmic dynamics that meet up again in the physical world. We are not privy to the starting point of our karmic relationships, which began before this earthly existence. But when we encounter difficult or unfinished relationships, it is easy to fall into the illusion that we are meeting for the first time. There is no such thing as "the first time." Few prayers are as difficult to say—and live fully—as asking for the grace of a truly generous heart: the capacity to perceive another person with a wide-angle heart-lens, reminding yourself of the higher mystical truth that you have no idea where this cosmic thread that you two are living together began. But meeting up together is yet another opportunity to untie that thread this time around, if your heart and soul are strong enough. It takes grace to untie a karmic knot—the ego cannot do it. The ego always falls into the illusion of vengeance or self-pity or anger or injustice.

Lord, grant me the grace of Generosity in my heart. I admit I may not be ready for the consequences of this grace and may even block its influence at times. I suspect I will recognize the power of this grace because it will open me to recognizing in others the same wounds I carry. And with that clarity, I will make more generous choices.

53

A CALL to PRAYER

Prayer

I AM IN WONDERMENT TODAY—holy wonderment. Very few human beings know that I seek Your company each day, that I crave my time for holy listening. And only very few know how deeply I believe in the power of prayer or how much I believe prayer can heal the cruelty and suffering in the world. Mystical power can heal the unhealable. I received an e-mail from someone today who tells me he thought of me while listening to the prayers of an imam in Bosnia. He tells me he thought of me during this "call to prayer." In fact, he recorded this "call to prayer" and sent it to me. A holy man calling people to prayer, doing just what I myself feel called to do, in my own way, all the time. I received a book yesterday on the rosary by a Buddhist who was visited by apparitions of the Madonna. He wrote that he was instructed by the Madonna to pray the rosary, and so he began to do just that. And now he has initiated rosary groups around the world. He calls the rosary "Mary's garden of roses"—and for him, praying the rosary is entering the garden of mystical roses. All of this holy wonderment came into my life in a single day. None of these individuals know I am writing about prayer, much less that I have decided to share about my personal prayer life with You. But they shared *their* prayer lives with me, openly and without hesitation. And my new Buddhist friend admitted with great joy that the Madonna directly inspired him. I find that so easy to believe. So easy. I imagine some people, perhaps most, would dismiss his claim of a visitation from the Madonna as nonsense. But she has a style, a *modus operandi*. And his story bears witness to Her holy style—that quiet way in which she shows up so unexpectedly into the life of someone. Often it's someone deeply in turmoil—which primes rich soil in the soul—and craving contact with a sacred experience capable of melting through the titanium wall of the reasoning mind. I needed a lot of time with You today, Lord, as a result of the deluge of all the prayer messages that poured into my life. I could not help but wonder, *What are You telling me?* And then I knew: You are calling humanity to prayer. It's not just me. And You're not calling us to church but to *prayer*. You are calling people to return to their holy roots and their mystical nature. You do not dwell in a church or a synagogue or a temple or a mosque. You are the entire Universe—a mystical, holy, organic force of light encompassing all life. Your nature is expressed in the mystical laws. You speak through all the laws of life: consistent, ever present, ordered, reliable. You are the Phoenix that assures us we will always rise from our own ashes. That is how You have designed the nature of life. And now You are calling us to pray: to direct the creative power of our souls into those high acts of grace that influence acts of creation. I tell people, Lord, that if energy medicine is cologne, grace is perfume. And that perfume can heal in ways that the ordinary mind cannot comprehend because the mind is so burdened by reason; it only considers what is *humanly* possible. But the soul dwells in the impossible and the miraculous. If only people dwelled in their souls, how differently they would envision their lives. I suspect that is why You are calling us all to prayer now: because we must imagine our lives differently, starting today.

Guidance

For all the many ways people imagine God, I have seen many, many people maintain a childlike belief that somewhere out in the cosmos exists an off-planet, father-like God who will somehow save us from ourselves. If we should do the unthinkable and enter into a nuclear war, this off-planet paternal God will somehow intervene—maybe make the bombs evaporate, or perhaps send a legion of angelic messengers to pull back the insane world leaders. But that is just not how heaven works. If it did, holy teachers, scriptures, saints, and spiritual teachings would never have been necessary. But our choices *do* matter. They determine our future. We are the engines of the events that are created on this Earth. The laws of creation say that our actions create consequences—and that we must experience the consequences of our actions. That is the dynamic of creation. Period. Like any dynamic in your own life, if you do not introduce better choices, you'll get the same lousy results. Prayer, however, is not just a better choice. Prayer is *the* choice. It is how we inject grace into any situation. I emphasize the phrase "inject grace" because, unlike ordinary choice and intention, injections of grace are mystical light. They blend *holy* intention with *your* intention. Prayer is your way of *choosing* God's help—but you still have to do your part. God isn't just going to fly in from way out there to clean up after you. You have to put some skin in the game of survival too. In this case, that skin is called your soul.

Grace

The grace of Faith is perhaps the most powerful of the graces. Without Faith, we become empty shells of ourselves. Without the capacity to believe in something greater than ourselves—even in our own higher potential—what is this life about? Life becomes reduced to an experience that begins and ends, nothing more than a moment of birth that unravels until the last breath. Grabbing stuff becomes the goal, even though in the end, you'll die no matter how much stuff you have acquired. I would believe in God for no other reason than this: not believing presents an unbearable portrait of life. Even the benefits of doing good or being kind are fleeting, brightening the day but leaving the soul starving after dark. We need Faith—if only to believe that every positive action we take, no matter how small, matters in some way. And we need to direct our faith into prayer, into mystical, silent dialogue with the Divine. And it *is* a dialogue, a deeply holy one that is heard and always returned. *We* matter in ways that defy reason and earthly calculations. Heaven does not measure our value by earthly productivity. It is not a corporation counting profits. It calculates acts of Faith, love, charity, forgiveness, kindness, trust, and compassion. This is your true currency. Believing in that one holy truth—that we do matter—means that regardless of how dark the moment we are enduring is, there is guidance hidden within. There, we find holy companionship, and a way through.

Lord, grant me the grace of Faith, most especially when
I cannot find it within myself. Help me hold on to the impossible,
especially when I am facing my own limitations. For this is when
I must rely the most upon what I cannot see or understand.

54

HOLY IMAGINATION

Prayer

THE OLDER I GET, LORD, the more I marvel at how you designed us. I am deeply enchanted by and in awe of the capacity of my soul to imagine what my mind cannot comprehend. I sometimes just observe the way my mind works. Left to its own devices, it wanders back into my history—rummaging through the mysteries left unsolved. Wondering why things happened as they did and reviewing unfinished conversations. It's often not a pleasant experience, Lord, except when I go back to collect wisdom. What did I learn? What will I never do again? I am not sentimental about the past, Lord, and I have few attachments to it. But I do want to gather the knowledge I have gained from my life and put it to good use. And it seems that knowledge and wisdom are currency in my soul. They fuel my liftoff into visionary altitudes where I can dwell in wonder about what is unfolding in the world below. In my soul, I can comprehend the fluidness of creation and how rapidly humanity can collectively shift an outcome. That is our power. Yet we fear intimacy, so we collectively push away the truth that we are one mystical body all breathing together. The Buddha saw this. Jesus taught this. But somehow it is the ultimate threat to our five senses. And so, we live in physical bodies in which we are constantly communicating to our cell tissues to act aggressively toward each other, that we are one another's enemy. The message we transmit to the planetary community is identical to the one we absorb in our physical bodies. We just cannot manage to live the truth that *what is in one is in the whole*. So simple. So obvious. And yet, so terrifying. We could heal so many illnesses in an instant by uniting the power of our soul's imagination and grace. If only we were not so afraid of our own wholeness, and that same power in others.

Guidance

I believe that many, many of our problems would be resolved if we would utilize the imagination of our soul. Imagination does not mean something is not real, as in "You are just imagining that." Imagination is the ability to "image" that which your physical senses cannot see. How you use your imagination is, of course, up to you. Some people imagine horrible scenarios, as we know, and some of them cross the line and act them out. But other people, like inventors and visionaries, open themselves to receive images of "incoming" forms—ideas, concepts, and possibilities— that need to be shepherded through the birth canal into reality. My experience with holy imagination is that our soul, unlike our mental abilities, is not bound by reason or logic. It doesn't need to know why things happened to us as they did. Our soul resides in the present moment, in the here and now. And it is capable of receiving insights and resolutions to obstacles that our minds could never conceive of. We are educated to rely upon logic, history, and familiar problem-solving routines. And because we are often ashamed about or humiliated by the problems we have in our lives, we are reluctant to approach—much less discuss—the problems we must resolve. Such feelings can lead us into a cycle of depression and despair, the exact opposite direction from resolution. The soul, on the other hand, is a vessel that gravitates toward the grace of hope. All things are possible with the help of the Divine. As the Buddha so often taught, circumstances can shift in a second. Nothing remains the same—ever. Not even the most unbearable circumstances.

Grace

Hope is like the water of life, a grace that lifts the burdens off our backs. Hope reminds us of the truth that all things change. And that, as Teresa of Ávila always taught, "With God, all things are possible." This is not our world; this is God's world. We did not make the rules. We are one species of life among hundreds of thousands. If we saw through humble eyes, we could see God everywhere. That is the true practice of Hope.

Lord, all I need to do is remind myself of the brevity of my life—compared to the infinite length of life itself—to buoy my sense of Hope. Nature is stronger and wiser than human beings. We may think we control nature at times, but we do not. We control nothing that matters. We cannot control life or death, or the cycles of nature, or the order of the planets, or the length of our own lives. Our own limitations fill me with Hope that You are indeed in charge of this Universe. That with each dawn, creation unfolds anew. Help me keep the grace of Hope ever burning in my heart.

55

HOW *Differently* WE SUFFER

Prayer

WHEN YOU SET ME ON this path, Lord, I knew nothing about healing. Perhaps only You and I knew the truth: that I wanted nothing to do with the world of ill and vulnerable people. Why You put me in the middle of that world was a mystery to me for years. I asked You to grant me some insight, some reason why you gave me the skills to help people—but did not include the appetite to do the task. I felt conscripted into service, and You know that. But You also knew I could not turn away from knowledge. Especially knowledge of the soul. How could I have lived so long and not known about its healing power? You put me on a path to discover everything I could not imagine: the interior map of who we are. I have noticed something, Lord. Something subtle, but oh-so-powerful: the way people are suffering has deepened through the years. I believe that inner suffering has become a pathway into a person's soul. Human suffering is no longer only the result of loss, loneliness, tragedy, or physical pain—though these remain ever present. No, suffering has gone deeper, reaching into the caverns of the soul. You lead a person into the inner sanctum through prayer, once they've made the choice to finally confront truth. The suffering I am witnessing is both emotional and mystical, personal and impersonal. I see it in the eyes of people, in their inability to name the reason they feel so imprisoned in their depressions. This is the suffering of our collective transformation, a soul-pain shared. It is untreatable but not unreachable. You are weaving us together, like it or not. If we cannot consciously embrace our oneness, we will bleed ourselves together. It is astonishing how we prefer to suffer apart rather than love together. But the sufferings we are enduring today have one thing in common:

they are the result of feeling separate from the whole. Whether we are enduring depression, loss, or survival-level fear, this feeling of separation now envelops so many of us. I know aloneness is Your way of beckoning us to meet You in prayer, to inevitably find You. In the breakdown will come a breakthrough. Soon, very soon, a calm will arrive. Fortitude will drop in, like manna from heaven, assuring us we will somehow endure. Inevitably we will wonder about the source of that sudden calmness, so needed in that exact moment. And we will consider, perhaps for the first time, the mystical truth that we are so carefully watched over, even in the midst of the darkest passages of the human journey.

Guidance

We human beings have always longed for proof of God to present itself in the immediate resolution of the burdens and injustices of life. Unfortunately that will never happen. Again and again, the greatest of spiritual guides—Jesus and the Buddha—have led us to look directly into the depths of human suffering. To rely upon our souls to cope with what our minds—and often our hearts—cannot bear. Their messages were not that suffering would eventually end, or that somehow God got human design wrong by including pain in it, or that justice could be found through enough acts of vengeance. Their teachings consistently directed their followers into the mystery of transcendence, into the mystical power of the human soul. Physical experience is fleeting. All experiences are gone the next day as new ones take their place. We have to struggle to hold on to even a horrible memory. We have to keep repeating our stories, again and again, or store them away deep in our psychic tissue. Otherwise the nature of our soul is to shed the shell of our painful experiences and retain the pearls of wisdom they produced. We are not meant to carry broken shells around with us. There is a logic to the mystical order of creation. There are choice and consequence, cause and effect, action and reaction. And we can track the creative power of our own choices and consequences. We can reflect upon our actions and reactions. We are creative engines, participating in so many of the dynamics that happen to us. There is no God that attacks us, but we often attack our own life. Waking up angry, for example, is an attack on your own life. Living in a state of anger is an energetic choice that has powerful consequences. Acts of betrayal have similar consequences. Whether you betray another person or your own integrity doesn't matter. Betrayal is betrayal. *Emotional excuses carry no weight with the laws of creation.* Consider the law of gravity. If someone pushes you off a building, you will fall, whether you are sad or happy about it. Emotions have nothing to do with how gravity works. Heaven is the same way. It is not a parent; it is a governing system of laws, choices, and consequences. And it is time we shed the burden of believing that life was meant to be easy, just, fair, or anything other than what it has always been. Life is a journey of choice and consequence, action and reaction. Whether you navigate it by faith or fear is up to you. And this journey of life has now become soul sized, embracing all of us.

Grace

The grace of Fortitude feels like no other grace. It erupts within you like an explosion of unfamiliar courage, as if companionship from afar has arrived. Fortitude speaks to you in its own voice, and it doesn't say but a word or two. Just enough to lead you through the darkest moment.

Lord, grant me the grace of Fortitude, especially when I am haunted at night and meet my weakest self and deepest fears. It is then that I need Your companionship. I may not be able to see You, but I know in my soul that I am not alone.

56

I KNOW I WILL HEAR
from YOU TODAY

Prayer

I EXPECT TO HEAR FROM YOU each day, and I am never disappointed. But I am always astounded—utterly astounded. A prayer will be answered, or I will sense You around me. I might notice something in my garden—something I see every day—only today it will suddenly seem unusual. Like so many other times before, I will pause and marvel as some hidden quality in this tree or that flower emerges. You are endlessly revealing Yourself in this world to us. Teresa of Ávila said, "Look for God in the small details." How I adore her wisdom. You are in the smallest details of our lives, every one of them. How could You not be? You are all creation itself. What is not You? The Buddha taught that separation was illusion, all illusion. That is a truth so big, so enormous it's difficult to grasp. And yet there is no truth more liberating. I often observe You melting Your way into someone's life, quietly disrupting their orderly existence. So many people do not recognize that when chaos sweeps into their lives, it means You've come to call in a big way. I often tell people that human beings are not talented enough to create the types of problems they are now facing. Only You could do that. Only You can initiate a person's complete transformation, just like that. Only You can bring a person completely to his knees by calling home his spouse or child. It's true, Lord; you pack one hell of a punch. And there is no arguing with You and no way to fight back. I've tried and lost every time. I've just had to accept the way life is. Age and death come to us all. As do birth and joy. And love and friendships. At least the nature of life is fair; I'll give You that. And You never fail to answer prayers—never.

Guidance

For me, the Divine has become as much an organic voice as it is a mystical one. There is nothing in life that is separate from all that is sacred and holy. All is part of the nature of God. Viewed from that mystical altitude, all life breathes and speaks and prays and heals together. What is in one is in the whole. The mystical laws of the Universe are living, breathing tools of creation. *Prayer is the intimate language of the Universe, the holy voice through which we co-create the world.*

Grace

Quietude is a state of grace that comes as a blessing directly from God. Quietude was described by Teresa of Ávila as a deeply mystical experience in which a person is overcome by a profound inner tranquility. This state goes well beyond that peaceful feeling you get when you are no longer worried about something. Quietude is a *mystical* state. Teresa seemed to suggest it transcended the boundaries of our five senses, bringing the individual into a cosmic state of bliss. She noted that once she was returned to her body and mind, the grace of Quietude remained within her for quite some time afterward—an active light that continued to nourish her soul.

Lord, I will light a candle in my own soul with this prayer and wait in silence for You. I ask for the blessing of Quietude in whatever way I am able to absorb its grace.

57

HOMELESSNESS

Prayer

HOW ODD, LORD, that I would have a conversation today about homelessness. It was with a man who was visiting the neighborhood. I could tell he was a very kind, good man. He was also so very old school, someone who believed that *every person had to pull their own weight in this world and that's all there is to it, by God.* I got what he was saying, Lord, and I will say I felt rather proud of myself. In my younger days, I would have gotten into a serious word battle with him. Instead I was able to speak from a compassionate place about the suffering in society today—and he was able to hear it. I could feel my heart open to him, and I could feel him relax into the conversation. He admitted not everyone was equally able to care for themselves. I wanted to download a cosmic view of what is now unfolding, Lord. In that moment, I could feel my head, my soul, my being spinning with the depth and width and magnitude of this moment of transition in which we are living. No, this is not "a homelessness problem" we are facing. Charity is no longer a solution. We are embarking on a journey into a new era and a new planetary community. We have entered the zone in between time and space, energy and matter. We are the generations who are exiting the old world, yet we have not quite entered the new. We are the generations who will see the evaporation of our national boundaries and our currencies and our familiar ways. We will not live to see the new world emerge—at least not in these bodies. Homelessness and refugees will explode in numbers, not diminish. This time will test our humanity to the max. Some may retreat into the illusion that we can go back to the old world and stop this evolutionary transition. But it's far too late to slow down. Our intuitive intelligence is always evolving and expanding while our energetic nature is taking charge of our biological design. We have crossed that Rubicon. So, which will it be, Lord? How will we decide? Will we enter into the power of our soul or retreat into the darkness of our fears? That is what You might well be wondering—but of course, You already know.

Guidance

Guidance is a funny thing. Do we ask in the privacy of our prayers and thoughts for insights on how to maneuver back to our past or through our present moment? Or are we seeking insights into the world yet to unfold? What motivates our prayers for guidance? So often we are prompted by fears—fears about what we anticipate might happen but rarely does, like becoming homeless. I long ago recognized others' brutal responses toward the homeless as their way of attacking the grim reaper of homelessness itself: a way of keeping the dreadful experience from coming into their own life. "I work hard," these people declare to the Fates. "Therefore, stay away from my door." Do people believe that homeless people *want* to be hungry, on the streets, stripped of their dignity? Or that refugees *want* to be far away from their homes and loved ones, living in complete uncertainty? These times are testing our souls, not just our wallets. All our fears about survival will come to the surface. For the mystical truth is that we are all one, and that truth is speaking to us through every circumstance we encounter—from homelessness to the good and kind acts we initiate. When we ask for guidance these days, it should be with the understanding that this journey of life is not a solo one. We all should pray each day: *What do I need to know or do to best contribute to the whole?*

Grace

Clarity, clear sightedness, is a grace that comes upon us as a sudden crystal-clear lens. In that instant, that which we did not see or understand a second before is revealed to us. But not in a way that validates that we are somehow the winner in an argument and the other person is wrong. This grace is one that brings a Clarity that transcends the needs of the ego and, rather, shines a light upon resolution.

Lord, grant me the grace of Clarity, most especially when I forget the truth about this life. It is so easy and comfortable to just think about myself. But a planet full of people only thinking about themselves is no longer spiritually sustainable. We must become better at this business of being human and spiritual.

58

THE MAJESTY *of* BIRTH

Prayer

I SAW A NEWBORN TODAY—a brand new, freshly delivered soul from heaven. Her mother was holding her so tenderly, so lovingly. I could tell she was amazed that she had brought a human being into the world, grown right inside her own body. I love that You send angels to escort souls on their descent into physical life. And I am grateful that we are given angelic escorts back to our spiritual home when the time comes. I recall so clearly, and so often, Lord, how my father glimpsed his angel escorts in the days before he left us. I found comfort in that, even though my heart was breaking at our imminent farewell. This physical life is so temporary. It goes so fast, a mere blink of the eye—though once we arrive we forget that. And so today, as I looked at this sweet new baby, all bundled up and ready for the adventure of life, I wondered, *Who is she, Lord? What will she do? How many lives will she influence? How much love will move through her over her lifetime?* Oh, all the many things that one human being can do. We are marvels, really. I wonder how You came up with the human design, and what other creatures like us are living out there in this vast Universe of Yours. We simply cannot comprehend the vastness of You. It's no wonder some people prefer to simply decide You don't exist. Actually, that's easier to believe. You are just too much to take in, too much to comprehend, too much to squeeze into our small human minds. Most people can't remember where their keys are most days, so how could they possibly comprehend the nature of You? Personally, I am content with my small encounters with awe, the mini-mystical realizations of the true majesty of each second, each molecule, each breath of life. I find You in the smallest details of life, hidden in all that is truly astonishing. Like the arrival of a new human being. It is utterly majestic to me.

Guidance

You may not realize how much we need to be in the experience of awe. We need to be "awestruck" by holy light, hit from within by that sudden sense of intimacy that we are known, watched over, and—dare I say this word—loved. It's not "love" in the human, sentimental sense. Rather, I'm talking about love of a cosmic, impersonal, but deeply real variety. "Unconditional love" is a popular phrase, but most only relate to it as not being judgmental of others and not being judged ourselves. That doesn't come close to the sense of love that is transmitted from an encounter with holy light. Imagine being born and raised in a dark, filthy, smoke-filled dungeon, never having seen daylight or breathed fresh air. Then one day you manage to find a door you had never noticed before and you push it open. There you are, standing in fresh grass on a lovely summer day. The sky is a rich blue, dotted with gorgeous ice cream–like clouds. The air is fresh and fragrant with flowers. You become dizzy with wonder from the sight of this sparkling new world. Every molecule in your body goes into exhilaration, suddenly finding itself in the atmosphere that maximizes its well-being: fresh air, light, clear water, warmth. A second later, the door closes, and you are back in the dark, dismal, filthy dungeon, fighting for your survival. Only now everything has changed. You try to tell people that another world exists and you found a way out. That there is a door that leads to a wondrous universe beyond description. Only no one believes you. You have discovered that the experience of awe—of the Divine—*is not transferable*. It is given directly to you, *for* you and only you. But now you know where you belong. You also know that you must return. One encounter with holy light, even for a second, is enough to make you seek it out again for the rest of your life.

Grace

The grace of Awe is nectar to the soul. We crave being in the state of Awe. We seek it out in all sorts of ways, thinking that sunrises, sunsets, ocean views, climbing to the tops of the highest mountains, or diving to mysterious places below the sea can somehow stimulate Awe. And they do—but only for a second. The grace of Awe, on the other hand, remains in your soul like a sweet fragrance, filling all your senses with an altered reality—no matter what you are looking at, no matter where you are standing. All life becomes an expression of the Divine. In that sudden realization, there is no other grace in which to dwell but Awe.

---

*I know I am seeking the grace of Awe because I am still
seeking, Lord. Something is missing, and that something is that
You and I have yet to meet. I have yet to sense You in that way
that takes my breath away and replaces it with grace. But I hold
Your prayer in my heart—seek, and I will find.*

59

ENDURANCE

Prayer

LORD, I NEED TO PRAY WITH YOU, to ask for guidance on matters that baffle me. Bafflement is not the most comfortable thing for me. People often ask me to explain why things happen as they do, and I never seem to be able to provide the answer they want. So many people want to know why things are so difficult for them or those they love. And to be honest, that is precisely my prayer to You today. Usually I can resolve that question myself. I do not have a child's view of this Universe, or of You for that matter. I dismissed Your being a "father figure" a long time ago. Still, I know You to be ever present, no matter how difficult the moment or the situation. I have had to ask You for the grace of Endurance many times before. And more than once, I have wondered how I ended up in the midst of a particularly frightening circumstance. Yet no matter how difficult things got, I did not wonder what You were up to. I only wondered how to maneuver through. I knew I had to endure each experience. I am not an exception to any of the experiences of life, no matter how deeply I believe in You. I am long past imagining that life should work out fairly or easily for me or my loved ones. I don't pray to convince You to change the nature of life for us. You certainly did not make life a cake-walk for Jesus or the Buddha. Their teachings were all about how to endure the challenges, the inevitable pain of life. And how to avoid adding to that pain through unnecessary suffering. Jesus did endless miracles, always teaching how the power of heaven can and does manipulate the laws of the universe on behalf of us because of faith. I have learned through the years, Lord, that much suffering in life is optional. We do not have to be angry or hateful or vengeful. We do not have to be deceitful or selfish or stubborn or dishonest. Such choices lead to more suffering—that's all there is to it. We can only blame ourselves for the consequences of our own dark behavior. Until we get that truth and live it fully, we will need the grace of Endurance. We need Your help to survive the suffering that comes from our need to think we are extraordinary, special, and not a part of the whole.

Guidance

It is obvious why you would need the grace of Endurance to sustain you through the experience of caretaking for a family member or navigating an economic transition in life that brings up survival issues. But few people ever consider how much they require the grace of Endurance to help get them through battles with their own inner shadow. How many times have we thought, "I just hate myself because I said that," or "I know I could have been kinder, but I wasn't"? We feel horrible about our actions and we promise ourselves that we will do better the next time we see this or that person. Meanwhile, we have to cope with the fall-out, and the guilty feelings our behavior activated in us. Often we make a promise to ourselves that we will do better next time. The truth is, there is nothing easy about the inner struggle with our shadow—nothing. It is a relentless force, and the source of so much self-generated suffering. Breaking our shadow patterns takes a devoted commitment to ourselves to truly do better next time—and mean it. And we need to endure our own failings, especially when we really are committed to becoming our better self. The grace of Endurance does not just provide holy sustenance to those caretakers who sit beside the beds of those in need. This grace supports us through whatever it is we must endure—including our own failings—along the spiritual path.

Grace

Who doesn't need the grace of Endurance? We cannot run away from what we are called to cope with or whom we are assigned to care for any more than we would want our caregivers to abandon us in our time of need. Said caregivers will have to endure our weakness and our suffering too. And how grateful we will be when this precious grace is bestowed upon those whose Endurance we are counting on.

Lord, grant me the grace of Endurance, not just for me but for others. Remind me that I will one day need to be endured: that one day I will be weak, old, and frail. Life is an investment of my energies. I am learning that more each day.

60

THE REALITY *of* SAINTS

Prayer

A LOT OF PEOPLE DO NOT BELIEVE in saints, Lord. Can't say I blame them. I bring this up today because I think I met someone who is one of those quiet, hidden people with the makings of a saint. I think You have modernized Your template for saints. You no longer hide them in monasteries. You are calling people to the rigors of selfless service everywhere. I recognize grace and holiness when I am around it, and this woman has the imprint. I certainly did not mention my thoughts to her. I never would. But I was deeply touched by the way she has designed her life around caring for the helpless and the homeless, including animals. She told me some outrageous stories about trying to get help for this person and that person. Each story sounded like a chronicle of heaven moving all forces on behalf of those who serve in the world. Only once did she say, "I swear I had the help of heaven on this one." That was the day she left her wallet at home only to realize it after ordering to-go meals for five homeless people. They were waiting in the parking lot across the street from the restaurant, watching the door for her to walk out with their meals. Realizing she did not have any money, she was about to ask the manager if he could trust her long enough to return with the funds. But just then— before she had revealed anything about her situation—another woman put a $100 bill on the counter. "Allow me," she said, and walked out. Telling me the story, this saintly woman laughed. "You know, I think God chose me to help others because I need so much help myself," she said. "The woman who paid for those five meals did not know I had forgotten my wallet! For some reason, she just smacked a hundred-dollar bill on the counter and kept walking. She didn't even wait for her change, so I gave it to the homeless guys for their next meal. Somehow things just work out whenever I am trying to get something done for others." She left me breathless with that last sentence, Lord. It was as if she was channeling grace—the living proof that heaven sends messengers to help those who are intent upon helping others. I felt so blessed to have met this person.

Guidance

Life is a paradoxical journey. I have so many stories of these extraordinary miracles—and they *are* miracles. But I have just as many stories of people waiting, as if in a long line, for their miracle to come along. I've been asked many times to "explain why God has not shown up." And the truth is that I cannot. I have no idea why a human being (or an angel) was sent to pay the bill for five hungry, homeless people one day—while thousands upon thousands of other human beings, including helpless children, wander hungry on our Earth. I don't know, and I have spent more than my fair share of hours wondering and praying and waiting for guidance on that question. But that is a human, logical question. It assumes that God's job is to compensate for all *we* could do for each other but choose not to. We could share more, we could fear less, we could hate less, we could do a better job of recognizing the humanity in all human beings. We're just not that good at it yet. When someone rises to the challenge, it still astounds us. We think of them as exceptional, perhaps even saints. But such compassion for strangers should not be so rare. It should not manifest in us only during times of extreme need, such as catastrophic floods or other disasters. In an ideal world, compassion toward those in need would be second nature, something that arises out of our hearts because the suffering in one person is in all of us. Sadly, the truth is that we fear the suffering masses. We avoid the pain we see in strangers because deep down we know their suffering could well be ours. Just like that the circumstances in our lives could change and we could switch places. The thought is too painful, so we avoid it altogether.

Grace

Compassion is not a mental force; it is a grace. Compassion calls us to act in ways that baffle our reason. Compassion does not weigh the scales of what a person *should* have done or *could* have done. Compassion dissolves self-righteousness and moves us to act as we would have others treat us in our moments of greatest need.

Lord, I need the grace of Compassion—and the grace of courage to let Compassion do its work on me. What good is Compassion if I try to control how much I feel and toward whom? I have to confront my fear of opening my heart to strangers. That's something I do indeed fear. My heart is accustomed to recognizing those who already dwell within it. Opening space for strangers is another matter entirely. I honestly do not know if my heart is able to carry the weight of those I do not know. I am at that crossroads. But what else can I do? Close my heart? How can I pray for anything if I am afraid of love?

61

PRAY LIKE YOU'RE *Crazy*

Prayer

WELL, NOW I'VE DONE IT, LORD. You really need to find someone else for this job. More and more people are asking me how to pray. I tell people to "pray like they're crazy." I tell people to talk *as if* You were listening—which sounds a lot like talking to themselves. I tell them to not think of You as Santa Claus, the great cosmic gift giver. For in truth, You are the great hidden resource. Human beings are just not used to Your style, how You maneuver via grace in the background of our lives. I told one person to pray, "Find me a way out, Lord. And watch over me through the night. I could use a peaceful night's sleep." I told him to avoid giving You advice on how to work the problem out. To trust You to handle the details. Human beings fear surrendering to You. We can hardly ever say a prayer of surrender. This, as I point out, is a funny way of proving how much faith we *do* have. We fear You are hovering somewhere out in the cosmos, waiting for us to say the dreaded word "surrender." We're worried You will sweep down and take our earthly resources. As if. What You *will* do is reorganize the mayhem and the madness we're already living with. Which can seem like adding more mayhem and madness, at least for a while. But inevitably Your way is the way *through*. I tell people to pray like they are crazy, like they have nothing to lose but their fear. If that's crazy, I'll take it.

Guidance

I'll tell you what's crazy: Holding on to pain and trauma that should long ago have been healed or released. Maintaining patterns of stress that only serve to break down your health. Continuing behavioral patterns that are fundamentally destructive. *That's crazy.* Surrendering your problems in faith to the Divine is not crazy; it's cosmic liberation. So set your soul free. Pray like you have nothing to lose except your fear. I have said this to so many people and have watched them recoil in fear at the thought of releasing their fears to You. Why? Because they realize that their fears are anchoring them to the world they know. They can tell that one prayer of surrender has the power to catapult them out of their suffering. Yet so many lack the faith to pull that lever. And so they retreat into doubt, with its darkness and suffering. They demand proof of what will happen if they surrender to the Divine. But faith does not work that way. Faith is the power to walk into the unknown. And let's face it—what *isn't* the unknown? Do you honestly know what is going to happen to you tomorrow? You think you do, but you really don't. You have no idea. None of us does. We can only hope that our world remains familiar to us. The truth is, we live in a continual state of surrender, only we are not conscious enough to realize it.

Grace

Wild Faith is more than Faith. It's Faith with abandon—bold, outrageous faith. It's Faith that says miracles are not just possible—they happen all the time.

Lord, I need You—and I need You now. I need help and I don't care how it comes. Just get it here. I need guidance. Download something into my soul ASAP. I release everything to You, and I am listening.

62

WHAT IS REAL?

Prayer

THERE COMES THE MOMENT, LORD, when we must realize how limited we are to help another person. Much less heal them. We do what we can, but the rest is up to You. I see this truth more and more, especially when it comes to the suffering people endure within the depths of their own consciousness. We've gone beyond the boundaries of the mind now. We are wading through inner space, like astronauts exploring the cosmic landscape of the soul. Who knows what we have stored inside us? How many secret portals are we opening, perhaps to past lives—or even to future ones? I know the soul is the timeless part of ourselves, residing within this temporal form. We are time and timelessness, body and spirit, energy and matter. Perhaps, Lord, that timeless dimension of ourselves, that inner sacred terrain, will take centuries for us to comprehend. My observations tell me that human suffering has upleveled a few notches recently. I am watching more and more people lost within the vast landscape of the inner self. I see them unlocking reservoirs of darkness they cannot—or do not realize they have to—explore in order to heal. Is that the role of sacraments and holy rituals? I am wondering anew about our need to bless and protect the unseen part of ourselves. We are not even that good at caring for the parts of ourselves that we *can* see, so I should not be surprised we have no idea how to attend to the needs of our soul. I am dearly close to one such person, someone I have known and loved since she was born. I have watched her journey further into her darkness year after year, growing increasingly unable to find her way back to the here and now, to this present moment, to the voices all of us can hear—including one another's. She told me, Lord, that she can no longer tell what is real and what is not. The experience of her physical life is real, but she has shifted her center of gravity to the timeless dimension. I can see that. What she is experiencing there is not the same kind of "real" that occurs in physical time. Tragically, she cannot discern the difference. Her awake time and dream time are colliding. This condition, Lord, is considered an illness. But is it? Is experiencing timelessness an illness? Are we afraid to identify what this experience *really* is, for fear of entering into the mystical phase of medicine? These people, through their anguish and pain, are leading modern medical researchers into the ancient domain of the sacred, if only indirectly. Of this I have no doubt: The day will come, Lord, when the physician will prescribe prayer and contemplation for the healing of the inner self. It will become clear that soul illness exists and prayer is the only medicine that works.

Guidance

Reality is a very fluid word, for reality is subjective. We do indeed create our own "realities." In my world, for example, the color lime green is banned. I *loathe* that color. It does not exist on my personal micro-planet. No harm comes to animals on my planet Earth. And absolutely no littering—to an obsessive point. All of us have made up our rules for life on our own micro-planets. And beyond the rules of behavior, cleanliness, noise level, and maintenance of physical order, we have also decided what we consider to be *real* in terms of the experiences that can and cannot happen in life. The purely scientific mind, for example, does not accept that anything can happen outside the laws of science. That position automatically assumes any mystical experience is an aberration or a hallucination. I remember having dinner in the mid-1980s with a Russian scientist who grew up under the Stalin regime. She had risen to a prestigious position as a professor of chemistry. She was known for her atheistic views, which she often spoke about in public. Then she had a near-death experience as a result of a serious car accident. While dead for a minute, she left her body and encountered the Divine, as well as her angelic guide. She felt flooded with love and awareness of the presence of the Divine everywhere in the Universe. She told me she was given instructions to return to her body, along with the caveat that she must leave her academic work and become a healer. She said that for weeks, she walked around the university feeling as if she were being stalked by an angel. She was terrified to tell anyone what she had experienced for fear of being diagnosed crazy and losing her job. She laughed when she added that she had a reputation for being ambitious and aggressive. No one would have ever asked her for help—or even considered her someone to confide in—much less asked her to *heal* them. But after her NDE, students began to approach her not for academic help but for sorting out personal problems. She told me she felt cornered, as if "something up there" (she could not bring herself to say the word "God") was determined to get "its" way. Then she got so ill that she had to take off a semester. During her illness the university brought in a superstar who was only supposed to stand in for the semester but instead took charge of many of her responsibilities. Next thing she knew, she was out of a job and, by necessity, on to her calling as a healer. She had been called from her scientific world into the mystical one. A collision of realities had occurred during her NDE, and finally she began her work as a healer. Our inner and outer realities are colliding these days. I see it all the time in the lives of the people I meet. And we can get very lost along the way, even to the point of wondering what, exactly, is real.

Grace

The grace of Trust is more than that small word conveys. Mystical experiences reshape your inner world into a place that few people can relate to, especially in this modern technical world of ours. We delight in fantasy television—fictional characters with imaginary friends and magical powers—because we crave the possibility that maybe, just maybe, that kind of power is real. Mystical experiences are not magical, but they are "otherworldly." You cannot bring proof to the masses that you have had a near-death experience, for example. You can only relate the tale of what it was like to be dead and to encounter a tunnel of light and a loving divine being. But you cannot *prove* a word of it. At the end of the day, you need to trust that you did, indeed, have that experience— even though no one around you has ever visited that reality. The grace of Trust fills you with the capacity to hold fast to what you know to be the truth, regardless of the skepticism of others or what the world tells you is or is not possible.

Lord, grant me the grace of Trust in my own inner journey.
Help me rely more and more upon my inner guidance
and Trust that I am hearing You clearly.

63

THERE *but for the* GRACE *of* GOD GO I

Prayer

I JUST WANT TO TALK WITH YOU TODAY, LORD. I want to tell You about my day. I feel like talking to You and sharing what has awakened in me. I remember hearing the adage "Except for the grace of God go I" over and over again as a child. I heard the nuns say it every once in a while. As a child I loved the sound of it. It seemed to hide a great jewel of wisdom. Almost like a treasure chest made of simple words that, strung together, communicated a powerful truth. "Except for the grace of God go I." Well, that truth exploded out of the dust of my memories today, Lord. It started out as just one of those days going nowhere—but ended up as a game changer. That's why I suspect You had a hand in it. Today was made for walking, so that's what I did. After a few hours, I got an iced tea and sat on a bench in the park to check my messages. I didn't pay any notice at all to the guy who sat down on the other end of the bench a few minutes later. Why would I? But then . . . he asked me if I would get him an iced tea. One glance told me, Lord, that he was homeless. I asked him if he wanted a sandwich, as long as I was getting him a drink. He did. I imagine You know the rest of the story, so perhaps my reason for telling you is to get the pain out of my own system. I turned to leave him as soon as I gave him his meal, but then he told me that he hated to eat alone and asked me to keep him company. I will admit to You that I was uncomfortable—I mean down to the pit of my stomach. But I was in a familiar park, and it was daylight. I also knew this truth: I wasn't afraid of *him*, I was afraid of his *pain*. So I sat there as he took one bite out of his sandwich and then one gulp of his drink. Then he started to speak. "I know you want to get the hell away from me," he said. "I know you are uncomfortable sitting next to me. You don't know me or anything about me. I'm a veteran. The war in my head won't stop. I just try to find quiet places now, like this park. That's all." My heart started to hurt, Lord. I could feel the pain in my chest explode. My eyes filled with tears, and then all I could hear in my head was "Except for the grace of God go I." Why him and not me? Why was I spared the pain this man was in? I could have been sent to war, forced to harm others or to face some other type of unimaginable horror—but I was not. Or I could have witnessed nightmares early on in my life, or I could have been a refugee. I could have had bombs drop on my home while I slept. But I have not experienced any such evil. I am not hungry, or without shelter, or without clothing or family or friends or hands or legs. As I sat next to this man, Lord, I felt the whole of my life reshape itself into a simple but deeply meaningful prayer of gratitude and grace. This man changed my life, Lord.

Guidance

As I sat on the bench with this stranger who shall forever reside in my heart, I could not help but become acutely aware that though we sat on the same bench in the same park, we lived in two vastly differently realities. His mind was filled with bullets and bloodshed and hunger and despair. I had the option of watching that on television—or not. He could not turn his inner television off, no matter what. The word *karma* seems to hold the secret to the mystery of the countless differences in our lives. But I don't know what to say about that. I don't believe the Divine does its calculations the way we do. Our lifetime is the only lifetime we can imagine, and so we put all our eggs in this basket. But what if we *could* imagine the vastness of our whole journey? How, then, would we value each lifetime? I don't know. And maybe we are prevented from that type of knowledge because none of it matters anyway. What matters is what we do for, and with, each other— in the here and now. Every day is a new beginning, a new gift. Imagine this truth: that every person you meet has the power to potentially change the rest of your life. How would you live differently if this were so? (And . . . it is.)

Grace

Sometimes we need to be reminded of the grace of Gratitude, and it is not always easy. Each day I become more aware of something I did not understand or realize before. I knew I should be grateful for all I have, but now I realize I should also be grateful for all I do *not* have. For all that I have been spared. I do not have traumatic war memories, and I do not have scars from being an unwanted refugee, and I do not have the fears of being homeless. There but for the grace of God go I.

I never know where I will find You, Lord, or how You will speak to me, and through whom. Some days it is through a stranger and at other times through a friend or a family member. Each time I am reminded yet again to be grateful for all I have—and for all I do not have. If I am grateful for having been spared, Lord, please give me the grace of compassion to help those who are suffering.

64

ANXIETY *in the* ATMOSPHERE

Prayer

I FEEL AWASH WITH ANXIETY TODAY, Lord, and I do not know why. I feel as if I am walking through an atmosphere that is pregnant with disasters. They might or might not happen; they could or could not be in the birth canal. My mind is unfocused, following thoughts and emotions like fractals of lights blinking behind my eyes. The clear guidance I am accustomed to—guidance that flows like a gentle, tiny, quiet thread of water through me—seems unreachable in this inner chaos. So I am asking You, "What is the source of these rumblings? How am I to interpret them?" Must we simply endure anxiety storms these days, as if each of us must process our own share of the overload of psychic free radicals in the atmosphere? Perhaps this anxiety is impersonal and all of us are tackling a small portion of it. We're an organic cleanup crew, each of us working on behalf of the whole, recycling our energy back into the collective. Maybe this is how the law "what is in one is in the whole" works. I can search all day for the source of this anxiety, but what would I find? What makes me anxious? I cannot abide noise, but my home is silent, so that can't be it. I have no significant conflicts to resolve, at least at present. Maybe something is bubbling that I do not yet recognize but that will soon make itself known to me? You have often alerted me gently to incoming shifts in my life, sending homeopathic guidance that enters my field of grace as a whisper before working its way to my conscious mind. I always sense that whisper. I know a message has been sent, though I can rarely interpret the content in the moment. Perhaps this anxiety is just such a message. Either way, I must still cope with this fractured atmosphere that is driving me to pace around my home. And yet . . . when I close my eyes and breathe deeply, imagining grace calming my whole being, the anxiety ceases. Puncturing through that giant-sized Buddha illusion, I have risen one vibrational level above the fray. Nothing in the physical world around me changes when I breathe grace into my body. Yet somehow I feel as if I am no longer in the grip of the lower atmosphere, as if I have tuned out the street noise and turned on Bach. I learn again and again, Lord, that this Universe in which we dwell is a wondrous creation, a conscious design of endless colors, sounds, and vibrational fields. The soul is our navigator through all that our eyes cannot see. Perhaps anxiety, Lord, is yet another way we must come into awareness of all that exists within the invisible landscape of our lives.

Guidance

It's so like us to seek out the reasons for what we are feeling and to look for a quick remedy to our discomfort. But what if the cause of our disquiet is not obvious and not ordinary? What if the epidemic of anxiety we are now experiencing is not rooted in something personal but something shared, something that has been generated from our collective soul? That's a thought that requires a moment—or three—of reflection. Consider the truth that all life breathes together. We are creatures of energy, and we are constantly expelling our energy into the atmosphere. Our energy blends together to create an atmosphere that, in turn, sets the energetic tone for the oxygen we breathe. We are becoming an increasingly anxious human community as we collectively sense and experience global changes happening at exponential speed. We live with an increasing sense of helplessness to make the changes our common sense—and our humanity—would direct us toward. We know many things are spinning out of control, from pandemics to environmental changes to politics to financial markets to the shifts in occupational security. As much as we would like to retreat into the stability of the past, that past is gone. We can only go forward. But without faith, wisdom, and courage, it is difficult to stand up to our fears.

Grace

Lord, grant me the graces of clarity, wisdom, and Courage in light of the many changes, obstacles, and illusions that fill the world these days. May I be directed through the chaos rather than into it. Change brings endings as well as beginnings, deaths as well as births. I do not want to resent or fear—or hold on to—all that must dissolve.

---

*Lord, grant me the wisdom to release what I must, and the
Courage to move into the unknown with faith that
I will be shown my way each day.*

65

FAITH *and* FAREWELLS

Prayer

IN THIS PAST YEAR I HAVE experienced a number of deaths of friends and family members, Lord, and I know there are more on the near horizon. I see their faces every evening. Sometimes waves of nostalgia wash over me as I recall my childhood and the years of my youth—and all the many family members who have passed on. Death would be unbearable, utterly unbearable, if I did not believe in an afterlife, Lord. Yet I do not believe in an afterlife *because* of that. I believe in an afterlife because nothing else makes sense of our spiritual life on this earthly journey. For what other reason would You bother with us? Why would the sacred world be so close, so intimate, so ever present if this were all there was? I do not know what the realm of holy light is like. Teresa of Ávila, the great mystic I so adore, wrote that her brain could not describe it, so she did not even try. She was left breathless and wordless upon her revival from a mystical journey. Something beyond the wonders of our limited minds awaits us and all of those who have gone before us. I take great comfort in that truth. I believe that not because I need a spiritual fantasy, though more than one person has hinted at that. I believe that because heaven has made itself known to me. Why would all of those interventions occur if this life were nothing more than, well, just *this* life? No, this life is a spiritual excursion into a densified form. Here we can sample, touch, see, and taste what we are capable of creating. The stage is temporary. It shifts by the second. Nothing is stable. We are living in a spiritual reality show. It's so obvious. It's also obvious that every choice we make is carefully watched. Nothing is missed. There is no need for You to interfere with even our darkest choices because we do not get away with anything. This truth makes life so much easier, even the most heartbreaking farewells. For even those are temporary.

Guidance

During my theological studies, I learned that God was everywhere and in everything. Now, however, my understanding goes well beyond that. *God is organic holy light, breathing life into the system of creation.* We cannot imagine the Divine or the workings of the holy realm. But nothing is more foolish than to decide there is nothing holy out there at all. There *is*. Fill in the blank any way you want. God, Goddess—whatever suits you. But never look up and imagine that you are not being carefully and intimately watched over. You are not alone. As one person said to me, "I'm not sure about God, actually, but it can't hurt to pray. I've got nothing to lose, so I'm going with that."

Grace

Comfort is a warm, glowing grace that fills you with a sense of inner security. It's the voice you hear out of the blue that says, "You'll get through this" or "This will work out." Divine Comfort comes in through the solar plexus, as the belly is the exact area where it's needed. When Comfort descends, the stress in your stomach calms down and you often feel the need to sleep.

Lord, grant me the grace of Comfort. If you could send it not only in times of stress but a little bit each day of my life as a precautionary measure, that would be deeply appreciated.

66

SENDING GRACE *to* THOSE IN NEED

Prayer

IT SEEMS I CANNOT TURN ON THE television these days, Lord, or walk down the street, and not see someone in pain or grief. Suffering is not a new condition for this world. When *haven't* people suffered? But it seems to me that the world is becoming a more intimate community now. Our technology, Lord, has finally caught up with what the mystics have known for centuries. The Internet is the energetic version of the "inner-net," the web connecting all of our souls. Sending prayers is no different from sending e-mails, really. Hit that internal "send" button and the light of a prayer is delivered to the person in need. I will always remember the person who told me she experienced the delivery of grace during a car accident. Having an out-of-body experience, she saw a person—a stranger—sitting in a car nearby, watching the accident and sending prayers. I loved the fact that she thought to look at the license plate of the car in which the praying stranger was sitting. Later, when she was healed, she located that woman via the license plate number to thank her for those prayers. Lord, I believe You wanted me to meet this woman so I would know that praying for others and sending grace were not useless acts of personal emotional comfort, but profound responses of love to a fellow human being. Though others appear to look different from us in the moment, everyone is really a part of our own soul.

Guidance

I suspect that when we die, we will discover there is no such thing as strangers or accidents. We simply cannot comprehend the organizational structure of this system of life. It's beyond our reach and grasp. How is it that we run into people we know, whom we haven't seen in years, just seconds after thinking about them? That happens all the time to many of us. Coincidences and synchronistic encounters tell us that the weave of life is remarkably intimate. And—no pun intended—thank God that it is. We rely upon holy intimacy far more than we consciously realize. That's the truth. We love the fact that we meet just the right people at just the right time, for example. And we are elated when just as we receive a wondrous inspiration, we happen to encounter a company that is ripe for that exact idea. We can brush this off as luck, but luck is a word for amateurs. The weave of holy intimacy is organic divinity at work within the fabric of life. We need to use those holy threads for the higher purpose of sending grace to others in need. We have entered the era in which we are about to discover the power of the "inner-net"—the greatest of which is our power to heal together through prayer and grace. We should strive to be *grace first responders.*

Grace

The grace of Compassion so often gets confused with pity. Compassion is not pity. The grace of Compassion expands the walls of the heart. Suddenly you are capable of understanding and responding to the suffering of others without harsh judgment, even when their behavior negatively impacts your life. When a reporter asked the Dalai Lama about his response to the Chinese soldiers who slaughtered hundreds of Tibetan monks, he said, "I feel compassion for them." The reporter was not just stunned by that response; he was disappointed. He wanted to hear the Dalai Lama speak words of vengeance and anger. He wanted an ordinary human response. But the grace of Compassion is not ordinary. It is a mystical force that defies ordinary choices and elevates us to the potential within ourselves to defeat our own dark judgments, which so easily arise in the face of what we disdain in the world. Yet we forget how easily the tables can turn. One day we may find ourselves hoping and praying that someone will look upon us with this powerful grace.

Lord, let Compassion flow from my soul to others, especially those in need, even when I am not praying for this grace. Keep a reserve of Compassion in my heart at all times. Help me be ever more mindful of my tendency to make negative judgments of others. Instead remind me—again and again—that I would not like such a judgment coming toward me. I would much rather be a source of light in this world, Lord, especially now.

67

THE DARK TRUTH

Prayer

WHAT KIND OF GOD WOULD CREATE such a cruel world? I cannot imagine how many times You have heard human beings utter that question, Lord. I hear it quite often myself when I'm teaching. For years I just told people, "This place isn't God's mess. It's ours." But I have to say, that was not the most enlightening response I've ever come up with. I did not want to tell them that I was still incubating my answer, that I was in the midst of that deep, long trek of unwinding my own dark passages so I could understand You. Why is it we make choices that perpetuate suffering and pain when we have so many choices that create the opposite outcome? Could it be that we are just more familiar with suffering? Or is the truth more brutal, Lord? Are we terrified to make loving and generous choices because those are the ones that liberate and free *others*? Is the deeper truth that we are genuinely terrified of empowering others with love and support? Are we so scared of loving more that we would rather suffer the result of selfish choices? Do we love as little as we can—just enough to survive? Love should be so easy, so free. But it's not, is it? Not really. Why is loving such a struggle when it is the one thing we crave the most? The truth is that love is also empowering. It is the substance that channels life and hope and wonder back into a human being, the same way oxygen revives a drowning victim. It's because it's so powerful that people guard love so judiciously. To love is one thing, but loving enough to empower another person? That is truly unconditional love. That's when cologne becomes pure perfume—the valuable fragrance that lasts. Love with conditions creates suffering. That's the dark truth. Love can disempower someone as much as empower them, Lord. Love can destroy a person as well as revive the will to live. We do not have to suffer at all, do we? Not when it's up to us to decide how deeply we will love others. But each person must confront whether he or she is able to love deeply enough to empower others, to liberate them to become whole beings. Or do we love in order to quiet our fears and insecurities? There are no secrets in this Universe, Lord.

Guidance

Power is a fundamental ingredient of the human experience. Everything we do, say, think, wear, buy—everything in our lives is a power calculation. Love is no exception. Love is perhaps the greatest power, more enduring than anger or rage or envy, because the power of pure love does not break you down. Love sustains you through the most difficult times. Dark powers like anger or rage will indeed keep you going and motivate you to all forms of actions. But those actions will take their toll on your life in one way or another. We hold on to anger because we believe someone has "disempowered" us. We tell ourselves we have a right to retrieve our power; that is how vengeance sounds in our heads. "Turning the other cheek" is advice we rarely follow; it seems, well, "otherworldly." There is no immediate prideful satisfaction when we turn the other cheek. We risk looking humiliated, as if we've lost the game—or worse, as if we've lost our courage. But the truth is that turning the other cheek is exactly what shatters the darkness and heals the deep, bleeding wounds of your heart. Choosing to see through the pain that drives the other person (or people), rather than hating them back, opens your heart. It liberates you from the grip of your own rage. When you do not return anger and rage to someone, you release yourself from the endless cycle of hatred and vengeance. You also free the other to move on, release their pain, forgive, and get on with the business of living and loving in the here and now. Holding on to wounds and hurt feelings is a choice. You are making *a personal choice* to dwell in the state of suffering. No matter how deep our wounds are in life—and some wounds are very deep and very brutal—in the end we have but one choice. We either stay bitter or we get better.

Grace

Healing takes the grace of Courage because it often requires us to excavate the depths of our own dark thoughts, fantasies, and desires. Wounds fester within us, and because they are poison they fill us with poisonous thoughts. We often embrace these thoughts because the idea of telling someone off—humiliating them or punishing them for hurting us—makes us feel empowered. But such actions never work—*never*. If we bring it up, those people will respond to us by saying, "What are you talking about? I never did that to you." Your pain is *your* pain—not anyone else's. And it's certainly not real to those who hurt you, any more than you can feel the pain you yourself have inflicted on others. No doubt you would deny how deeply you have hurt others if they confronted you; think about that. Everyone's healing is a personal journey, and that's all there is to it. It takes the grace of Courage to finally face that truth.

Lord, grant me the Courage to confront my own darkness, my own inner shadow, my own blockages to love. I may think of myself as loving, but the truth is that I love conveniently. I am afraid of the power of love. It takes Courage to be unconditionally loving. Help me open my heart beyond the boundaries of my own safety net. I have no idea what strangers or even foes might find their way into my heart. But unconditional love is exactly that: love without conditions.

68

HOW DO I TELL PEOPLE *to* TALK TO YOU?

Prayer

I READ A PRAYER POEM TODAY, Lord, and it enchanted me. It was about a squirrel and a patch of grass saying "Hey" to each other. The poet noted that he was saying "hey" a lot these days, too, because formality wasn't working so well. How do I tell people to approach You? Informal, holy conversation works for me—and it was this poet's way. I am not certain that our way of praying to You makes a great deal of sense to a lot of people. People often ask me, "How does God answer you?" They wonder if You appear to me or if I hear Your voice or float out of my body. How do I explain the subtle nature of holy guidance? I trust all that I cannot see. And this grace-filled atmosphere is alive to me. Teresa of Ávila wrote that we must look for You in the small details of our lives. One day that sentence made all the sense in the world to me. Just like that. One day the world became filled with small details, each a vessel of divine intervention. My imagination aside, I realized that this universe was fully, totally You. You were not separate—a Being "up there" hidden behind cloud cover. You were manifested in all that was created, including every person. In that instant, every person seemed wondrous to me, each a soul on an earthly journey. Some looked so lost and others looked elated to be here. In that instant, the invisible field was suddenly cluttered with angels tracking their human beings, keeping watch over them with such care. Heaven is not formal. It is intimate, loving, and ever present. If only those who felt lost or alone could truly know that, Lord. How very different they would feel. Everything about their lives would shift in a second. The choices they make would be bold and daring, outrageous and creative. They would wake up each morning and breathe into the prayer "Hey, what shall we do today, Lord? Talk to me."

Guidance

I grew up with Latin prayers and Gregorian chants. If I prayed then as informally as I do now, I would get a lecture or two (or thirty) from the nuns and priests who taught me religion. But they did teach me a deep sense of reverence—which I have not only retained but nurtured. I have learned through my own experience that the holy world is an intimate realm and it surrounds us. It is not above us; it is everywhere. The Buddha said that when we die, we take our actions with us, the sum of all our parts. We are responsible for what we have contributed to all of creation. Think about that. Life is a journey of responsibility. Why would that truth end with the death of your body? It doesn't. We are wired to hear our invisible support team, our holy guides. Prayer—not logic, not reason—is the route in. People want reasons and proof because they do not want to give up their relationship with darkness. They fear the light. Everyone should look at how much they fear a direct encounter with the light. Think about how much that would change your life—because it would. And that truth tells you how powerful—and how near—the light really is.

Grace

The grace of Wonder is a grace few people ever think about. Perhaps most people do not even consider Wonder a grace, but every attribute can be elevated to the power of a grace. The grace of Wonder lifts an ordinary thought into the holy atmosphere. Instead of saying, "I could never do that," you are filled with a sense of wonderment. And you find yourself saying, "Why *can't* I do that? In fact, I *will* do that!" The grace of wonderment evaporates obstacles. All you can say is *yes*.

*Lord, just the thought that this world is an intimate,
holy theater of life fills me with Wonder. But that thought
comes and goes. I cannot hold it. Grant me the grace of Wonder,
the experience of feeling the power of wonderment incarnate in my
blood and bones. I know that experience will change my life. The world
will become an intimate, holy place for me—and there is no looking
back after that. But it fills me with Wonder to wake up and pray,
"Hey, what do You want me to do with my life today, Lord?"*

69

MAYDAY

Prayer

I AM TREMBLING WITH TERROR and fear tonight, Lord.
I cannot rest. I cannot sleep. I cannot forget what I saw on the
news tonight, cannot bear knowing all these people are suffering
at our borders because they want a better life. My own grandpar-
ents came here as young teenagers because they wanted a better
life— and they were alone. But I also cannot fathom the hatred
immigrants are encountering. That hatred tells me more about
what is happening to the myth of America than anything else. If
Americans still believed in America, if they still believed that this
was a nation of abundance and dreams and hope, such hatred
could not thrive here. We could not be led by people who man-
ufacture lies like illegal drugs. For that is what they are: psychic
heroin, drugging the consciousness of a nation. Those who believe
the lies become available to the dark side; they become channels
for hatred. Lord, I recall wondering as a child when I read about
the Nazis pursuing the Jews, why did You not intervene? Why
didn't You just send the Angel of Death to grab their souls during
the night, a repeat of Passover? It worked the first time. I know
that's not going to happen—but please, intervene *somehow*. Send
angels and aid, pour mercy and compassion into the airwaves to
open the hearts of people. So many are possessed by fears that
they won't have enough, that immigrants will take their jobs and
their homes. Some people cannot bear to face the truth that this
world is changing, that You have other plans for the future of this
planet, including how (and whether) we live here. How is it, Lord,
that we still cannot get along? I do not even think that You sending a divine apparition like the Virgin of Guadalupe would change
anything today. I fear we are leading ourselves to encounter the

worst of ourselves. We might well end up destroying ourselves. That is why I am trembling with terror tonight. I know heaven is working overtime to wake people up. Suffering has always been the great motivator. But now it's madness and evil unleashed. When will it be too late?

Guidance

Everyone is feeling the chaos now. And if you cannot feel it in your psychic field, you can see it on television and in your town. You have to be residing in denial to not see the truth of how fast we have spun out of control as a global society. The source of this is so obvious: we do not want to share or change or accept our fellow human beings, to become a global community. Every crisis at its root is the result of the fear of other people—their color, their religion, their hunger. We forget how brief our lives are. None of us will take our goods and money with us. Stuff will not buy us one more second of life. All that matters in this journey is whether we lived by the truths of our soul and how we treated our fellow human beings.

Grace

Lord, grant me the grace of Courage. I don't know what I might face tomorrow or even later today. But these are no longer ordinary times. Every day holds the possibility of encountering a person who needs someone to speak up for them. What if that spokesperson needs to be me?

Hover over me, Lord, and fill me with Courage.
It is too easy to run for cover and pretend everything is going
to be just fine without my help. It won't. Nothing will be fine
unless each of us is willing to confront the darkness.

70

PRAYING *for* OTHERS

Prayer

I AM ALWAYS ASKED TO PRAY FOR OTHERS, Lord, and I do. My list is long and growing all the time. I know there is great power in praying for others. The grace is delivered to them, like a beam of light shining upon them from heaven. Jesus said, "Ask and it shall be given." And so, I am asking that the graces of compassion and mercy be poured down upon the refugees of this world, all those forced from their homes because of war or gangs. I cannot imagine the terror of having to flee my own home, the safety of this place I love. It is unimaginable to me. And yet it was probably unthinkable for all of them as well. Who thinks that one day they will be standing captive behind a barbed wire fence or in a cage, held as a prisoner because they feared for their life at home, only to find they ran toward another, equally threatening, fire? Lord, open the hearts and minds of people to the depth and horror of this crisis. Refugees embody what we fear the most: homelessness and vulnerability. But I know all too well, Lord, that if we do not help them—that if we do not learn the truth that what happens to one person happens to all of us—the world will soon become a residence of fractured human beings. Perhaps we need to rethink the meaning of homelessness and include what it means to be *spiritually* homeless. For we each require a spiritual home to turn to. I have spoken to people who were formerly homeless, and they have shared stories with me. They've told me how grateful they were to the few people who were not afraid to touch them, to offer words of comfort, and to promise to pray for them. In that instant they felt respect and dignity flow into them. Grace was channeled to them as they received words of comfort and the money for a meal. But I know in my soul, Lord, that it is You who inspires such encounters, who offers such profound healing to us fractured human beings. One prayer has the power to resurrect a starving soul.

Guidance

What is in one is in the whole. What happens to the least of my brethren happens to me. Again and again, the great spiritual masters have given us the teachings that we are in this life *together*. That each of us is a small part of the same collective experience. What will make us finally act, think, vote, and love by that truth?

Grace

Endurance has many expressions, and we need all of them. Endurance is a grace that helps us share others' burdens: it allows us to carry what is not ours to carry, sharing our strength and power on behalf of others. We choose to make room for others, but it's heaven that provides the grace needed for that loving choice.

Lord, grant me the grace of Endurance. I ask not just for myself but that I might find a way—through my own prayer—to carry others' grief and terror. I hold those who suffer in my prayers, Lord, and in my heart. There but for the grace of You go I.

71

SOUL CHOICES

Prayer

NOWADAYS I THINK ABOUT MY LIFE, Lord, as an endless excursion into the power I have to set choices in motion. How I dance with creation by deciding what to do with this life of mine. Little by little I am realizing that every thought I have, every breath I take releases sparks of creative energy—my energy, my grace— into this Universe. Every flash of love, or fear, or anger, or joy, or curiosity, or gratitude ignites a consequence. Every burst of energy starts the fires of creation, which blend into the forces of energy already in motion. That is what this journey of my life—everyone's life—is really about. What, then, am I creating with this soul of mine? I will have to account for my acts of creation when I leave this Earth. We do not get the gift of all this power and not have to account for it. This is far too orderly a Universe for our lives to be disorderly and unaccounted for. I suspect that when I leave this Earth, everything that seems so important to me here— everything I worry about—will crumble away. I will realize how utterly insignificant it was to not have enough of this or that, or how much pain I caused by holding on to anger or stressing out about whatever. I don't want to wait that long, Lord, to come to my spiritual senses. I want some wild and powerful grace to sweep through me and flush out my inner reptiles and fears. I cannot afford to be afraid of small choices anymore. I cannot afford to imagine fears that are nonsense, or concern myself for even a second about what others think. My only concern now is whether I am hearing You clearly. I have less time ahead of me now, Lord, than behind me. I do not want to be someone who is frightened of other people or carries darkness in my heart. If I am such a person,

I need to see that and heal it. My choices are far too powerful. I cannot afford a negative choice.

Guidance

If we truly realized the consequences of our negative choices, we would err on the side of love, optimism, trust, and generosity, if only to benefit ourselves. But the shadow in us—our pride, anger, more pride, more anger—can quickly get us into hot water. We do stupid things and we say stupid things. If only we realized we were creating our own suffering with the power of our dark creativity.

Grace

The grace of Trust—outrageous Trust—is an infusion of inner strength, clarity, and confidence. It makes you feel as if you can break through any obstacle before you, though you may not be certain how you will accomplish that feat. What you do know, with great certainty, is that you will.

I ask you, Lord, for the grace of outrageous Trust in You.
I want to see clearly, love fully, and have the courage to make
life better for even just one person—other than myself—every day.
I am so grateful for this precious gift of life I share with humanity.
Hover over me, Lord, and occasionally let me know You're there.

72

STORMS *at* NIGHT

Prayer

HOVER OVER ME TONIGHT, LORD. My soul is filled with chaos and my heart is filled with despair. I should know better by now than to fear the growing madness in the world, but sometimes I still get caught in the gravity field. I tell myself that we are passing through a cycle of transition, but I am also aware that transition brings destruction. I see how fear is changing so many people. Our survival sense is working on overdrive, telling us that the ground beneath our feet is shifting. We are getting subtle messages that tell us our familiar world is fading from view, yet we do not clearly see our new homestead. We're not even sure whether there *is* a new homestead. Absent from so many people are Your graces of faith and trust: in themselves, in this country, in the future, and ultimately in a safety net from You. Nothing surprises You. You are that which is always prepared, never surprised, always the known. And we humans are just the opposite. I was going to say, "Thank God opposites attract." Instead, Lord, I ask You tonight to send Your angels to lift the heaviness from my soul while I sleep. Wrap me in grace and let nothing disturb the silence of this night with You. I know that with You, all things are possible—including downloading the graces of hope and generosity into the hearts of people. This is Your Earth, Your world, Your creation, including all of us. Even the greatest of difficulties evaporates at Your command. Grant me the joy of inner silence tonight, Lord. Let me rest in the celestial realm.

Guidance

There is a gravity field of chaos generated by all the changes happening in the world. And we can get caught up in it, just as we can get caught in rushing floodwaters. A psychic sensation comes over us, dragging us into the darkest emotions. They instantly take hold of our own emotional field, contaminating our personal thoughts and feelings. Just like that we are out of touch with hope and optimism. And for the moment—maybe longer—it can appear that the dark side is calling the shots on this journey of life. Stay long enough in that psychic field and your energy begins to wane, as if the life force is being squeezed out of you. Lightness is replaced by an increasing sensation of "densification" as you gradually, perhaps even rapidly, become depressed from lack of light. It's not a personal depression, this fog of despair. It's like a visitation into the depths of collective psychic despair, the center of the spinning, magnetic vortex caused by our collective psychic free radicals. This zone is real. It's dark. And it belongs to all of us. Prayer gets you out of this place. You have to fill yourself with light that lifts you like a helium balloon beyond the vibrational grip of this vampiric energy. We've all been in this zone. We have all helped create this zone. And we can destroy this zone with prayer.

Grace

I think of the grace of Protection as a cloak of invisibility floating around me. No one can see it, but I know it's there. It's like an electric fence that burns up the energy of dark thoughts before they can get to me. I can hear them, certainly, but their capacity to grab hold of me or influence me is lessened. I also think of this grace as the fuel for my survival instincts. Something or someone may seem safe or trustworthy, but my gut will tell me otherwise. I have learned to trust this instinct much more than anything I see or hear. Protective signals such as these are pure grace and guidance.

Lord, keep me under the grace of Protection, now and always. You see what I cannot. You know this path that I am walking. Therefore, I must rely upon Your view far more than my own. Protect me through the days and nights of my life, Lord. Watch over me on the long path of my life's journey, today and always.

73

ONLY YOU COULD *Change* *the* WORLD SO FAST

Prayer

YOU CERTAINLY HAVE THE WORLD spinning on its axis, Lord. This virus has brought the world to a standstill. Just like that. I'm sure most people would have said a month ago that such a thing was impossible. But as Teresa of Ávila so wisely noted, nothing is impossible for You. Most people will credit the virus for this total disruption, and yes, the virus is the active and obvious agent. But it is not the *mystical* agent. There is always a mystical agent. I am sure some will say we are being punished; but they do not know You. Or at best, they still believe that You behave like a human being, managing a court of human law. I'm not yet sure of the higher reasons we have entered into this collective experience. I do know that for decades, we have been receiving the message that we must shift to wholism, that what is in one is in the whole. That we must become a planetary community. Perhaps now is that moment, and this is the way. We must heal our way into wholism in the same way individuals who need to heal find their way to a new consciousness. This is no different. It's just all of us instead of one of us.

Guidance

For decades now, we have spoken about creating our own reality. We haven't really grasped that "creating our own reality" is a mystical truth, not a behavioral one. Co-creation does not give us permission to do whatever we want. It demands that we become aware of the truth that every choice we make results in an act of creation. If we could realize the power of our soul, and unite with each other through prayer, we could heal this world.

Grace

Faith in yourself is the first step to truly realizing Faith in God. If you don't have Faith in yourself, in keeping your word to yourself, in believing in yourself, how can you have Faith in that which you cannot see or even imagine? Begin with the first step—develop Faith in keeping your word to yourself. Pray for the grace to do just that. As small a task as it might seem, it is not. And you will know the grace of Faith when you succeed in even the smallest way.

Lord, grant me the grace of Faith, most especially because it is so challenging. But not having Faith, even in myself, is living without a map. I have no idea what to do or how to make a choice. I can't trust my intuition. Faith is everything. It is my lifeline to You.

74

DOWNLOAD

Prayer

I CAN FEEL THAT SOMETHING—a message—has entered into my energy field, Lord. I sensed an immediate shift this evening. I want to acknowledge that I am aware that I have received a download, and I will wait, and listen, and let the message incubate. I know now that You are alerting me that something is going to change in my life. You are telling me to prepare. I am not yet certain whether You have given me instructions or are simply telling me to prepare to let go. But I am listening and waiting. This happens so often now. I find that I detach from everything in my life the instant I have that sensation. Everything evaporates, and it doesn't matter to me. And that astounds me. I love my home, and yet I could detach from it in a second. I sense the messenger and I prepare to pack my bags, as I have done before. After living in New England for 10 years, I packed my bags in three days. I had been gone from home for a month and heard the messenger You sent as soon as I walked back through the door. Immediately I began making arrangements to leave New England—even before I took my coat off. Twenty minutes after I received the download, the wheels were in motion for me to move. And I left two days later, back to Chicago. I have never not listened to the messengers You've sent. You are louder to me than ordinary sound. I don't understand it myself. Go figure.

Guidance

Everyone receives guidance. Messages are sent to us constantly. I am not unusual in that way. Except, perhaps, that I have always listened. And followed the instructions. I will admit that I have not always wanted to; I have frequently wanted to do something other than what I was being told to do. I remember once feeling as if I was in an actual fistfight with something invisible. Much later, as I thought about that moment—which I actually did quite often—I was awestruck by how physical that invisible force felt to me that day. Someone could speculate, of course, that such an encounter is imagination—and I do have a wild imagination. But it's not. I cannot prove—nor am I interested in trying to prove—how intimate the holy world is with our lives. It's up to each of us to decide how close to You we want to be, how *authentically spiritual* a life we want to live. What you have to understand is that the holy world is *this close* to you. It's not your choice to decide whether or not you are watched over. All you get to do is decide to live according to that truth or keep denying it. That's the only real choice you have. Remember: you did not design this Universe. The system was in place before you were born, and it will keep going long after you die. You were born into an eternal operation that is far greater than life on this little planet of ours, so trying to change the rules of eternity to suit this present-day "scientific and rational" mind of ours is utter nonsense. As you can see by looking around—it's not working out that well for us, is it?

Grace

Just when we think we know what's going on, or that we know all about some subject, we discover how wrong we are. Humility is the grace that reminds us we know nothing at all, or not quite enough, or we just aren't as right as we thought we were. The one truth we can count on is that the more we know, the less we know. And we will never, ever understand the mystery of creation. Nothing should have us walking more humbly on this Earth. As we recognize our vast limitations, we start to see the ongoing brutality of our own nature: that which we have yet to heal within ourselves. Still, after all these centuries, we cannot stop creating weapons to destroy each other. We are a long way from being as smart as we think we are. We would be much better off to retreat into our holy nature, our mystical consciousness, and approach the heavens with our shoes off on sacred ground.

Lord, keep me humble. How do I know what goes on behind the stars or beyond this galaxy? I haven't a clue. For all I know, the night sky is a veil hiding another world. I have no idea. I now realize that my ideas block Your guidance. Keep me ever mindful, Lord, of the grace of Humility. If I stop telling myself what I think is going on in this world, perhaps You'll download a few clues.

75

GRACE BATS LAST

Prayer

I HEARD THE WRITER ANNE LAMOTT tell an audience, "Well, you know grace bats last." And I *screamed*, Lord, right then and there, right out loud. I nearly flew out of my chair. The truth of that small phrase nearly blew me away. Anne is so onto You—but of course she is. Grace always comes in at the last moment. I've learned that You will use any means as a conduit of grace into our lives—strangers, friends, noble adversaries, whispers in the night, traffic delays. The door we least expect is often Your favorite entrance. Though You may be notorious for late entries, You always arrive—like the theater diva who requires a breathless audience. Who knows how many ways grace has come into our lives without our noticing? But then again, we live in the sacred field of Your breath. Rarely do we stop to think about that. And we certainly do not understand (nor can we, really) what it means to dwell within Your being, Your universe. This truth is the meaning of the mystical body of Christ: we are a mystical field of souls, bound together through holy light. But who can possibly comprehend that wild, wondrous truth? That's the wonder of the mystical realm, really. The slightest contact with You and the entire cosmos is revealed for what it is: a sacred playground operated by holy beings. I imagine there is wisdom in our forgetting that truth, in drinking from the river of forgetfulness before we incarnate. Who could behold such a reality and still manage to get to work on time? You have left us with that constant craving, however, for something we cannot find on this Earth. We crave awe. We long to have an encounter with the extraordinary, with the unexplainable, with the mysterious, with the sacred. And perhaps that is why grace bats last. We need to feel that longing and discover that nothing tangible really fills that emptiness in us. We must remember we are seeking something wondrous that we cannot explain, something that enters into our lives just when we need it to, right on time. We want to be left wondering, *How did that happen? Could the impossible actually be possible?*

Guidance

We really do love stories of miracles, divine intervention, and the visitation of angels disguised as human beings. I wrote my book *Invisible Acts of Power* as the result of asking people to share stories of receiving spontaneous acts of service from others. The approximately 1,400 personal stories I read, all within a week, changed my life forever—for several reasons. Most of all because I realized somewhere in the midst of reading all those stories that I was actually reading experiences of how grace manifests in our lives. And though no one ever suggested that they had encountered an angel, I knew I was reading stories of divine intervention. So many people shared stories of meeting odd strangers who delivered profound, life-changing messages—and then disappeared. One person, for example, said he was on his way home to commit suicide. While standing on a corner trying to decide whether to cut his wrists or overdose, he noticed that a car had stopped at the stop sign in front of him. Instead of driving away, the driver was signaling that she was waiting for him to cross the street. And she was smiling, he reported, "the warmest smile I ever saw." He decided to live one more day because of that smile . . . and one more day after that. Eventually he decided to just go on living. In stories like these, the handiwork of heaven is so obvious, so present. And the same is true in your life: once you learn to recognize the presence of grace, you will never feel alone again.

Grace

Wonder is a grace with so many meanings. You can be "filled with Wonder." And you can "Wonder when" something is going to happen. And then "something wonderful" happens—just like that. Wonder is a grace that can lift you right out of this moment in time, inspiring you to ask, "Now, what was I so worried about anyway?"

Lord, drench me in the grace of Wonder. Just to imagine this grace fills me with anticipation of something wonderful. Perhaps that feeling itself is this grace, misting my energy field. Hover over me, Lord, and keep me ever in the blessings of Your graces.

76

PROVIDENCE

Prayer

I NEVER HEAR ANYONE USE THE WORD *providence* these days, Lord. What a powerful, holy word to put into retirement. Providence makes me think of watchful care. We are always wondering, of course, what watchful care means when it comes to the eyes of heaven. I know that this is my life to live, and that I will fall off the edge of a building if I am careless. I take a risk; I pay the price. But I also know that prayer—and following Your guidance—form a working partnership with You. And the grace of providence goes with the territory. We are automatically under Your watchful care. The mystery is how that care appears. But I have also learned that divine care and human care are not the same thing. Perhaps that is why people so often want "proof" where You are concerned, Lord. They want heavenly intervention to solve earthly dilemmas. But You are like the teacher who observes the students studying long days and nights, trying to understand math or philosophy. A problem arises for a student, who then goes on a quest for the only book that has the knowledge she needs. You know where it is, but You say nothing. You observe her panicking as she goes through all the shelves in the library and checks out every possible reference. Still You say nothing. Finally, she collapses on her bed, exhausted, crying from confusion and panic, and she utters a prayer: "I give up. If You want me to do this, You'd better help me." One minute later there's a knock on her door. A friend just found an interesting book that she no longer needs and thought she might like it. And just like that, the book no one could find—the book practically no one had heard of—walks right into her dorm room. After that, my prayer for help, for divine providence in all matters, always came first and not last in my endeavors—that girl searching for that book in the library was me.

Guidance

I suppose a person could think of that book showing up as a lucky break, but I do not believe in luck. Why didn't that book show up earlier? Because then I would not have been so grateful. I would not have exhausted my own resources. I would not have said a prayer in which I acknowledged that without divine intervention I will fail. Because I depleted my own resources doing what I believed I was supposed to be doing—completing my education—I truly believed that God *had* to do something to help me. It never occurred to me, to be honest, that I would not get some sort of answer from the Divine. It never occurred to me at all that I would not be shown a way to resolve the issue that seemed the size of the world to me back then.

Grace

I think of Providence as an old-fashioned grace, perhaps because we rarely use the word anymore. But it is a word worth reinstating into your vocabulary so you may pray for the grace to flow abundantly into your life. Providence assures you that you are under the watchful care of the Divine. What a deeply calming message to receive.

Lord, keep me under Your watchful care. Grant me the grace of Providence in all ways. I think of this grace as our handshake, an agreement that You guide and I follow. This is the grace of our covenant, our partnership. Watch over me, Lord, and keep me and those I love and care for, friends and family, in Your care.

77

I CAME *upon a* SHAMAN

Prayer

I HEARD A MAN SINGING, LORD, and I followed the sound of his stunning voice to a park. I was nowhere near home. As I entered this little park I thought, *Who is this man with such a voice? And what is that hauntingly lovely song?* This young man was on his knees, arms raised to the heavens. He was singing to You, Lord. This man was a shaman, one of Your earthly ministers of grace. I thought for a moment that I should leave him alone in his prayer time with You; I was conscious that I was invading his holy ritual. But he noticed me just as I entertained that thought. He gave me a smile that told me I could stay—and pray—with him. His voice was glorious, and his prayer so beautiful. He was asking for a mystery to be revealed to him, something only You could tell him. In between singing his prayerful song, he beat a drum. I felt as if the surrounding trees and plants had joined him in his prayers to You. I joined him as well. I was swept into his field of grace, into his vortex of faith. I fell into prayer and felt lifted up on the sound of his voice. The grace he generated around him felt so rare to me, Lord. I wondered, *What is this extraordinary sensation?* Then I realized You were speaking to him—it was a holy current filling the air. He called, and You came. The grace of You was electrifying. All I could say to You was "Thank You." I know You answer all prayers. But I felt as though I was witnessing Your divine response flowing into the soul of a human being even as he was praying to You. Utter holy bliss. Then I watched him, Lord, as he relaxed into the Earth, eyes closed. The silent embrace of nature remained for a second. Then he opened his eyes, kissed the ground, and stood up. I didn't want to move or even breathe for fear of disturbing the sublime atmosphere, but this shaman turned around and nodded his head at me. I smiled and returned the nod. And we both walked away. I noticed a few people coming into the park as we were leaving. I was so tempted to say, "This place was just visited by heaven. Take your shoes off. This really is sacred ground." But then, what isn't sacred ground? All creation is Yours. Sometimes I am breathless with wonder. That is all I have to say.

Guidance

Though we may not consciously recognize that we have a need to experience awe, to come into contact with some expression of the sacred, we do. We have a deeply spiritual need to be lifted off the Earth by some contact, however brief or natural, with a messenger of the Divine. We need to feel—to know—that there is something greater than us beyond this life. We do not really need to know the fine-print details about the sacred; it is enough to encounter its presence. To be immersed for a microsecond in that holy Light that is beyond all light. We can tell ourselves that we do not need religion, and that's okay; I am not speaking about religion. I am talking about the Divine itself, which could not possibly squeeze into the container of religion. The Divine is the life that is Life itself, the light that is Light. We are drawn to that cosmic, holy substance because it is our purest substance. One encounter with Divine Light communicates the mystical truth that we are particles of that Light. We do not have to imagine it or talk about it; we need just allow those Divine particles of Light to animate within us, like sparklers. We long to experience that mystical state in which our sense of reason is anesthetized, releasing us to experience the realm of all things holy, grace filled, and eternal. We do not want to be imprisoned by reason and doubt, be it self-doubt or doubt about whether our life has value. But most of all, deep in our spiritual truth, we long to be able to raise our arms to the heavens like a shaman. To sing our prayers with complete abandon, never doubting for an instant that God will show up. There is nothing as powerful as a soul filled with faith.

Grace

It was the grace of unquestioning, unreasonable Faith that Jesus was referring to when he said that the faith of a mustard seed could move a mountain. We have become creatures of reason, driven by the need for proof and guarantees and immediate solutions. Faith in the Divine defies everything such reason relies upon. And yet there is that part of us that cannot help but wonder, and hope, and want to be blown away by an unreasonable, incomprehensible miracle. We yearn for fully miraculous intervention at those moments when we need God's help the most. We may doubt at times that a God is out there. And some may even claim not to believe at all. But a deeper spiritual truth pulsates in each one of us. (Loudly in some, and nearly on a respirator in others.) We cannot stop ourselves from hoping that some Presence—a power much greater than our reasoning minds can comprehend—is governing our lives.

Lord, I want my soul to sing in prayer to You.
Just thank You. Thank You. Thank You.

78

THE NIGHTS *of* FIRE

Prayer

LORD, I OFTEN THINK OF the teachings of Teresa of Ávila—
more than "often," actually. I think every day of something she
wrote. In so many ways, she speaks to me. Through her teachings,
I have understood the rigors of the spiritual journey. She so elo-
quently speaks to the paradoxical, unexplainable tug-of-war that
happens when a soul encounters You. How we then seek to experience that indescribable sensation again and again while fearing
it at the same time. My fear got the better of me not long ago. I
thought perhaps I could wander away from all this seeking for a
while, go on a bit of a sabbatical from my interior life. And then I
dreamed one night that I was standing outside the wall of Ávila,
Teresa's walled town in Spain. The wall was ablaze with fire. She
was standing inside the town calling to me, beckoning me to walk
through the fire. I couldn't do it. All I felt was fear, so much fear
I woke up sweating. I looked for her in my room, half expecting
to see her. Why do I even need to tell You this? I somehow imagine You already know. And so, You know I did not want to go to
sleep the following evening. I felt as if heaven was breathing in
my room, waiting to take me back into that living dream. And so,
it happened. Again I stood in front of the burning wall of Ávila,
listening to her command me to walk through the fire. Even in
the dream, I held my breath and ran, expecting to be evaporated
in flames. But the only sensation I felt as I ran through the fire was
bliss. I was running into pure Light, pure You. I felt as if every molecule in my body separated for a second and flew through the cosmos. I was stretched across time and space, eternity and mortality,
and then woven back together again. Except now, the fear of being
close to You was gone. Everything about life and being alive—the

ability to love so many and so much, and the gift of being alive with so many wondrous human beings—shimmered like a field of diamonds. The goodness and wonder of life showed itself to be so pure and so available. I would never have thought of goodness, kindness, and wonder as graces that are abundant and available. I experienced that truth and now I know it in my soul. These graces are like bubbles floating in the air around us, available to burst into our lives. We need only ask. So many holy gifts fill the air. We are living in a field of grace, bouncing from one grace-bubble to the next. If people only knew. They would live so fearlessly because they would no longer—*could* no longer—doubt You.

Guidance

I adore the teachings of Buddhism for so many reasons. Again and again, I experience the truth that the life we see with our eyes and hear with our ears is one big illusion. The physical world really is a stage, filled with carefully selected props and supporting characters. Each serves a specific purpose—teaching us what we need to learn about ourselves and the creative power of our beliefs. Yet our subtle fear of God influences how we see the world and the choices we make about our interior life. The fear of a mystical encounter with God may not be obvious to us. In fact it's been my experience that many people will not even speak of this fear, as it runs so deep. But another form of that fear is our fear of truth: of speaking the truth, of hearing the truth, of confronting the truth. Truth is the nature of the Divine. Truth is power. We take cover in denial because we do not want the illusions we hold dear to be revealed. One encounter with a truth can bring down an entire stage of props in a second. As the Buddha taught, life can and does change in the blink of an eye. Such change occurs as soon as the power of a truth comes in. And yet that power—that fire—liberates a person like nothing else can. Burdens are lifted from your shoulders even as the stage crumbles in flames. The spiritual journey is only about truth, and nothing more.

Grace

The grace of Courage is required as we explore the interior life. Facing our fears can feel like walking through a wall of fire. We fear being burned alive. Yet what is it that we fear so much? Surely being free of fear is the beginning of a new life.

Grant me the grace of Courage, Lord. I sometimes fear losing everything I have. I fear losing my family, and I fear being consumed in my own fears. And yet, I long to be free of all these fears most of all. I dream of tranquility and peace, of finding a place in the world without fear. In my quiet moments, I know that the only true place of peace is within me. So I return to that place again and again. And I always find You waiting in that stillness. You are the constant.

79

A HEALING PRAYER

Prayer

TODAY, LORD, I WILL keep in my heart the many people who have asked for prayers for healing. I do not know how You distribute healing grace or how the mechanism of healing works for those who ask. We all need so much healing. I know You pour out your healing grace abundantly. And I also know there is no end to the pain and suffering of this human life. I have wondered so many times whether, if we all prayed together—I mean all of us—the world might experience a massive healing. For those suffering because they need shelter, grant passage to a safe home. For those suffering from disease, grant the grace of healing. For those in great turmoil, grant the ability to hear Your guidance. For those coping with loss, grant solace in mourning. And surround this planet with grace, Lord. Pour it into our environment, wracked as it is with pain and abuse. This beautiful Earth, this stunning, living creature that provides for all of us, is enduring so much. I don't have to tell You that, Lord. But I have to say it, to acknowledge the need for grace. Lord, keep watch over this Earth—this life of ours—and each of us who calls it home.

Guidance

I have never met a person who does not need the grace of healing in some way. We are a curious species in that the strongest part of us is invisible: our soul. The mystical truth is that we are all a part of one soul, one inner-net. As Jesus taught, what we do to one, we do to all. When we pray for one person, we are participating in healing the whole of humanity. For the world to change, we must all journey together. No one is on this planet alone.

Grace

Divine Healing is the grace that Jesus channeled so freely. Knowing he was a conduit for this grace, he healed people effortlessly. We fear this grace as much as we desperately need it. An instant Healing or a Healing of a terminal illness brings us into direct contact with the mystical realm—the holy unexplainable truth that we belong to the sacred. What could be more terrifying—and comforting—than that?

Lord, may the grace of Healing be poured abundantly unto all living creatures. May that holy grace ease the suffering of humanity and this Earth and bring us ever closer to living as a loving community, without fear of sharing—or of each other.

80

ON MERCY

Prayer

I RARELY HEAR PEOPLE SPEAK of mercy, Lord. But for some reason, I paused during Mass the other day and considered what it meant to ask, "Have mercy on me, Lord." As I reflected upon the grace of mercy, I realized that it is a subtle, exquisite grace. How is it we experience mercy in our everyday lives? It occurred to me as I dwelled on this grace that we must give mercy to receive it. We cannot be given something that we do not give freely and openly to others. I held that thought in my heart as I left church. I wondered what circumstances in my life call for mercy. You know how many times I have asked for the graces of patience, fortitude, compassion—my list is endless. But I have not asked You for mercy. Is that because I have thought I do not need mercy? Does such thinking come from my own blindness to the consequences of my actions upon others? I don't want to think so—but perhaps there is truth to be found in the examination of this question with You today. Self-examination gets tedious at times, I have to say. And yet, I find that I am compelled to examine mercy more deeply. I wonder what happens within us and around us when You pour mercy upon our lives. I read a story that remains alive in my heart, a simple story, really. A man wrote about being sent to the Gulag in Siberia. He was starving on that long train ride. A guard accidentally dropped a piece of bread. The prisoner spent the day, the entire day, waiting for the right moment to grab that piece of bread. Finally he thought the moment came and he bent down and reached for that small piece of brown, rotting, dirty bread. And the guard saw him. He said his first reaction was to pray that You have mercy on this guard, that You would soften his heart for just a second. He said that guard looked at him, looked at the bread, and said, "Go ahead. Take the bread." The guard took mercy upon him. Though it was hardly enough for a meal, he said that somehow he was no longer hungry. He felt full. Full not just with bread but with the gift of humanity, the gift of mercy. I think that's what mercy feels like. Maybe we are the engines of mercy here in this life. As we do to others, so You return to us.

Guidance

For all the many ways people have described themselves to me in workshops—loving, strong, stubborn, compassionate, energetic—never in all my years has someone said they were a "merciful" human being. I myself would not have said that either. The grace of mercy is perhaps that obscure. Or the word itself feels somehow "old world" to us. But I encourage you to think about the power it carries. In your life have you ever been in need of mercy, such as a merciful judgment in court or a merciful act of forgiveness from someone you've harmed? We so often judge each other, especially those whose behavior strikes us as extreme. But what do we know of the many experiences that created such behavior in a person's life? Our judgments have consequences; that much I know. May I remember that truth and nurture a merciful heart.

Grace

Mercy is a grace we need in massive supply. Do not think of Mercy as the decision to grant a more benevolent judgment upon someone, though that is certainly an expression of Mercy. This grace weaves through your life in ways you cannot imagine. Consider the merciful act of the Divine *not* allowing something to happen to or for you that you thought was so right for you. A very wise spiritual teacher taught me that it is a merciful God who prevents our foolish decisions from incarnating into our lives— lest we do more harm to ourselves and others than we could ever in our reckless innocence have imagined. Emphasis on *reckless innocence.* Mercy is an extraordinary—and I might add, highly underrated—grace. One I would recommend reintroducing into your heart.

Lord, I am ever more mindful of Mercy now. This grace is with me, especially in the privacy of my thoughts. I have no idea why people do what they do or act as they do. It is a Mercy to be released from wanting to know. Lord, grant me the grace of Mercy as a living presence in my heart. And may the Mercy I show to others be bestowed upon me in times of need.

81

DISAPPEARING NATURE

Prayer

LORD, THE DISTRESS IN ME is bubbling up like lava from a hot volcano. If ever I needed You to calm my nerves, to download some inspiration, to lift me off the Earth and into that holy atmosphere beyond this moment of life, it is now. Right now. I am hearing so many stories about the abuse of the Earth, working my way through the badlands of the foolish, horrid, wretched decisions people make. And then there are days like today, when news of the slaughter of the Brazilian rain forests makes me want to scream from helplessness. I am screaming at You, in fact. I want the destroyer in You to come out. I want You to send down Your army of killer angels, as You did to free the Israelites from their time of slavery in Egypt thousands of years ago. Why not? Wouldn't that wake up—and shake up—a few people? Why have You retired Your armed guards? I've long wondered about those great biblical stories. Did they happen? Did they not? I've cycled through different thoughts on the Old Testament stories. Some days I think they are fabulous myths, and *Who cares if they really happened?* Other days I wonder, *Mmmm, what if those stories are true? And if so, why were You so present thousands of years ago?* I think You *were* present, Lord. I don't think those ancient Israelites were imagining the parting of the Red Sea, or the Angel of Death passing over Egypt one fateful evening. I think the difference between then and now, those ancient people and us, was the way they believed in You—and the *era* in which they believed. It was a time of silence on the Earth. A precious time, really, in which human beings existed briefly between heaven and Earth. Doubt, reason, the scientific mind, logic—all such blockages to the mystical, invisible world—had yet to be constructed. Their reliance upon

You was as dependent as their reliance upon water, air, and food. Today we have no idea we are still dependent upon You. We've fallen under the spell of our own minds. We think we can slaughter at will and that there will be no consequences to our actions. You have given us choice, Lord. And as such You are going to let us fall on the sword. That is the panic I feel. We could so easily make other choices, but greed has a way of making a person think he can outrun death itself. Perhaps You are sending the Angel of Death once again, only this time it looks a lot like—us.

Guidance

I often hear people say, "Why doesn't God *do* something?" I've wondered that myself, more times than I can count. But the rules of life are that *we* are the engines of creation. We influence the events of our personal lives, and we participate in the creation of the greater events that shape our world. There is no off-planet God who is going to sweep down here at the last moment and save us from our foolish choices. We will live with the consequences of our choices, as brutal and horrid as they might be. That is the reality of the gift of the power of choice. And that is the consequence of denial and passivity, of believing that the unthinkable cannot happen because it has not *yet* happened. But this is the age of the unthinkable, of unprecedented actions and choices. That also means we can make choices unlike anything we have ever considered before. We have never considered the soul to be a powerful change agent. We have never united in prayer to break through barriers of collective negative thinking. Prayer is not a religious activity. It is a soul power, a cosmic force. It is the intimate sacred language of the celestial realm that unites us all.

Grace

Grant me the grace of Courage, Lord, so I may rise up when needed. So in difficult times I will not take cover in denial. I am alive now, during a time of great chaos and change. I am not meant to be an observer but to participate in this journey of transformation. I cannot expect others to carry the weight of my life on their shoulders while I tell myself everything will be fine. Nothing will be fine unless we all join forces to create a healthy future. You will not undo our foolish choices, but You will enhance our courageous ones.

Lord, inspire Courage in the hearts of humanity, now more than ever. It is one thing for a few people to feel adrift, but we are a global community spinning into the unknown. Only You could turn the world upside down so fast. You would never release this power into the hands of a human being. You are speaking through nature, through something organic. You are ever so present in this crisis, Lord.

82

MORE THOUGHTS *on the* GRACE *of* PROVIDENCE

Prayer

HOW MUCH OF LIFE IS "MEANT TO BE"—and how much can we control? How much of our lives have You already determined and how much is up to us? I have wondered about this so often, Lord. I have also considered in deep reflection whether I really want to know the answer. To be under the grace of providence is to be under Your protective care in all ways. I was educated by the Sisters of Providence, nuns dedicated to the grace of providence. They relied upon this grace and inspired us with their experiences of miraculous interventions: food arriving just when they needed it and other forms of assistance. The message was clear: Your intervention occurs in the second it is required. Not a moment before—because it is not required in that moment. You will bend the laws of nature and reorder a person's universe if necessary, if it is the only way through. But if there is a human solution, a miracle will not happen. Miracles arrive only when they are essential. Yet providence guarantees that You will always guide a person to a human solution. This grace is intimately woven into the workings of nature. I have learned that's what makes it so unique and mysterious. Yet part of that mystery is how, if we have taken the wrong path, it can feel as if You have abandoned us in the forest at night. At those times I wonder if that darkness is a test—or if it's just what it feels like to be in the waiting room of my own life. Perhaps it is simply a resting zone that I am misinterpreting as a wrong turn in the road. We are creatures of action, after all. People are always telling me about synchronistic experiences they believe to be signs from You: signals that let them know they are on the right path. Sensing You around us in some way—in *any* way—is how we prove to ourselves that we are under Your providential care. We want to feel that we are wrapped in the grace of providence, a grace we may not even be able to name. We seek proof that You are watching over us. And, You are. In spite of all the disbelief I hear, Lord, and the struggles people have with faith, it takes nothing more than a divine coincidence for doubt to fall away. Suddenly they feel they are on the right path. They are breathing more easily in their skin because they have had a sign that they are dwelling under Your providential grace. Now if they could only remember the feeling of that grace, the power of that grace, the next time they feel lost in the forest at night.

Guidance

I ponder the nature of God often these days. Among the many thoughts that take me down deep into the quietude of my soul are these: *Why do some lives seem so guided, while others do not? Why are some saved, while so many others die in tsunamis or massive explosions or refugee camps? Are we not all under divine protection?* I finally realized that there are no logical answers. Life is ultimately a mystical experience, not a trip to court. Heaven does not work like the human judicial system, seeking all things to be right and just. I can no more figure out heaven than I can describe the width or depth of the cosmos. Yet in spite of the paradoxes, the Divine remains consistent. We can rely upon the order and the workings of the natural laws. We will all die many times and in many ways over the course of our lives. And we will each rise up as a phoenix, every time, whether we want to or not. Our spirits will spark back into life, no matter how many times we fall down. That is the promise of our nature. It is an expression of the benevolent, loving nature of the Divine. We are designed to rise again, to recover, to try again, to love again, to reach out to life, and to look up to the heavens for grace. We are designed to be under the providential care of the Divine, even down to the promise that we will always spring back to life, even after the darkest winter.

Grace

Providence is that powerful grace that falls upon you to ensure that you will be where you need to be, when you need to be there. Your life has a plan and your soul knows the route. Your mind gets impulses, ideas, and thoughts inspired by your soul. Everyone's map needs to be rerouted at times due to life circumstances. That's when we must rely most upon prayer, trust, and guidance.

Hover over me, Lord, even when I forget You are in my life.
Keep me in Your providential care, now and always.

83

Through DIVINE EYES

Prayer

LORD, I'VE MADE A DECISION, one that comes from contemplating my endless pursuit to be doing something, anything. Doing nothing has always represented uselessness to me, like sleeping in too late. I have forbidden myself to do either since becoming an adult. But I have recently begun to examine my inability to pause. I have wondered if my refusal to ease up is because I fear being of no use. What is the scale upon which we measure our value, anyway? After long, long days of reflection on this matter, I've made the decision that I will not betray the gift that is my life by thinking I am of no use—no matter what circumstances I find myself in as the years of my life go by. I may not always embrace the responsibility for finding ways to be of use, or the circumstances in which I find myself. It is up to me to participate with a full heart and a willing spirit. On those days when my spirit is not so willing and my heart is not filled with kindness, I ask that You shine Your light upon me. I know that life is much fuller, much richer when I sense Your grace at my back, like wind in my sails. But I will admit that on the days when I feel lost at sea, I sometimes forget that no matter where my boat sails, I am always on Your ocean. So, let me ask that You find use for me each day that I have life—in Your way, not mine. My part will be not to judge how You have put me to use. I will assume that even just sitting next to a stranger on a park bench or standing in a line that's far too long is of use in some way. I need only see it through the eyes of my soul. I have already had so many experiences of viewing my life through my soul that it stuns me when I still falter, when I still slip into ordinary sight. But I do, again and again. Yet, again and again I have experienced that seeing through the eyes of my soul makes everything look different instantly, as if a black and white photo shifted to color in the palm of my hand. People look kinder, softer, and more vulnerable. I find I am less inclined to judge anyone and anything, and I smile more easily. The truth is, when I view the world through divine eyes, I become saturated in wonder. I see it as Your creation, all blending together. Nothing and no one appear out of place or without meaning and purpose. It doesn't matter that I have no idea where all the pieces of life belong. I am one of those pieces, just blending in.

Guidance

The difference between how the soul *perceives* your world and how your eyes *see* your world is like night and day. Your soul is tasked with rigorously peeling away illusions and guiding you to discover your inner senses—the part of you that intuits truth in a way your physical senses cannot. We base our values and our self-worth on what we believe to be true and real in our world. We often say, "Seeing is believing." That is unfortunate because faith is all about believing what you *cannot* see. And so much of your value, so much of what you do to make a difference in this world can only be evaluated by the Divine. Accumulated acts of grace, such as kindness and patience, generosity and noble strength, give life and hope. You may never see the long-term—or even short-term—effects of the thousands of acts of grace you generate each day. But lives are changed because of that grace. View life through your soul and you'll understand that there is no such thing as a small or powerless choice. If you truly open the eyes of your soul, you'll see that the Divine gives you at least one opportunity a day to make another person's life just a little better. And should you be that someone in need of assistance, look through your soul. You'll discover heaven hidden in the small details of your life.

Grace

When do we not need the grace of Clarity? This powerful grace creates the sensation of a fog lifting from within. Either suddenly or gradually, slowly or instantly, you become clear-sighted about the thing that previously weighed so heavily on your soul. Grace, remember, always calls you to action. From Clarity comes choice. Grace never lets you sit still for too long. It's a change agent. Why else would you need it?

Grant me the grace of Clarity, Lord. Allow me to see the world as my soul sees it. Clear-sightedness comes naturally to the soul. Our holy interior perceives truth without distraction or detachment. Our soul has the ability to see our life path. It turns our attention away from getting our own needs met and toward asking how we can make others' lives better. Lord, again and again I am reminded of how very brief this life is, and that it is not about accumulating stuff. Life is about how well we tend to all that lives. That is all that matters. And no act of serving life is too small.

84

THE FOREVER MYSTERY *of* FAITH

Prayer

"HOW DOES GOD HELP?" "What should I do after I say a prayer?" "What signs should I look for to know that my prayer has been heard?" Lord, those are the questions I was asked during an interview recently. I could tell from the questions—and from the look in the eyes of the writer—that she was asking them for herself. Her inquiries had nothing to do with any article she was writing. So I asked her what it was she herself needed help with, and she said she was "working on faith." She wanted to know what exactly I trusted and had faith in. I could tell that writing the article gave her the courage to ask questions she would never otherwise have considered asking. Perhaps she feared You might just show up in her life, cleverly disguised as the winds of change or a sudden plague. But I also knew she desperately wanted to understand how it was possible to have faith in what cannot be seen or touched. I asked her if she had faith in herself, if she kept her word to herself or ever betrayed herself. She didn't answer, which meant yes, she had betrayed herself. And no, she had no faith in herself whatsoever. I told her it was pretty near impossible to have faith in God—a Presence you cannot see—when she had little experience of having faith in herself, the presence she dwells within 24/7. I suggested she begin her long sojourn into faith with herself. I told her to consider asking for grace when she felt herself tipping toward an act of self-betrayal. While I know she has yet to experience grace consciously, she will in her moments of prayer. That yearning for faith is so distressful for her that she does not realize that the yearning itself is rooted in deep faith. She wouldn't be so concerned if she didn't have faith that something greater than meets the eye is governing this life of ours. She simply has yet to recognize the mystery of faith and its organic threads that run throughout our web of life. But she will.

Guidance

We require faith and trust for our life to make sense to us. I have listened to so many people describe why they are depressed or anxious or unhappy in life. Often they refer to unresolved issues from the past or present-day stresses that seem to have no end date. No one has ever told me that their depression is rooted in a crisis of faith, that they suffer deeply from an inability to believe in themselves. And that as a result of that core dilemma, they cannot trust themselves or anyone else—much less believe in the mystical truth that their lives are divinely intended acts of creation. The absence of faith in yourself is like losing the key to the great treasure box of your life. You can buy lots of stuff and go lots of places, but the truth is that nothing you purchase and nowhere you travel can fill the black hole that comes from not trusting yourself.

Grace

When it comes to our inner life, the graces of Faith and Trust are inseparable; two sides of the same coin. Without Faith in yourself, it is impossible to Trust yourself. And if you cannot Trust yourself, you can never—ever—Trust another person. You will always be braced for them to disappoint you in some way because you carry that self-loathing that comes from continually failing yourself. Self-esteem is built with the hard inner labor of earning Faith and Trust in yourself, one choice and one action at a time. This discipline eventually becomes a devotion. Eventually the Faith and Trust you develop in yourself become the means through which you find Faith and Trust in something greater than yourself—the Divine.

How do I pray for the graces I need to earn, Lord?
Today I am praying for Faith and Trust. Somehow,
in some unreasonable way, I have Faith and Trust that
You will pour those graces into my soul even as
I struggle to earn Faith and Trust in myself.

85

Pure JOY

Prayer

I SPENT MUCH OF THE DAY ALONE, Lord, in quiet, reflecting upon this and that. And then in that moment of quietude, of deep prayer, I erupted with joy. This wasn't ordinary joy—this was the *grace* of joy. I felt joyous for no particular reason. Not because something happened or because I had just received good news. The grace of joy felt as if I had suddenly been sprayed with the most delicate, tranquilizing, uplifting fragrance that had the power to make my body feel weightless. It was utterly blissful. I did not want the sensation to end. I wanted to send this fragrance to everyone. And then it occurred to me in the midst of this gift of grace that I had never, ever instructed a person to pray for the grace of joy. Not once. It never occurred to me to pray for joy or to even think about such a prayer. But in the midst of that wonder, and now as I dwell in the reality of that grace, I realize, *What was I thinking? Why would we not pray for Joy, especially when we are in despair or going through difficulties?* Maybe other people like me have never thought of praying for the grace of joy. But if ever a grace was needed, Lord, it is joy.

Guidance

I rarely hear people describe themselves as joyful, or *joy-filled*. I'm not sure people think about what it is to be joyful, or the need for joy in their lives, but they should. *You* should. Joy is an exceptional grace: a grace that lifts your spirit beyond the boundaries of the ordinary emotions in which we dwell during our days. Reflect for a moment upon the range of emotions that are most familiar. For the most part, we live in the extremes: depression and anger on the one end, or excitement and romantic love on the other.

Neutral is calm, which means no active crisis at the moment. But living in joy? It's not on most people's radar. Joyfulness does not require a reason, or another person, or romance in order to exist. You can nurture joyfulness in any circumstance, simply because you choose to experience life through the grace of joy. It might be hard to imagine how a person could feel joyful while experiencing difficulty or tragedy. Joyfulness is not like light-hearted happiness or "party time." It is a deeply mature soul grace that defies logic and reason—as do so many of the events of our lives.

Grace

The grace of Joy blends with hope. It reminds you that you will make it through even the darkest passage, that life always renews itself. You may think you won't make it through. You may not even *want* to survive at first. But after a while, something will happen, usually something small. And it will bring Joy to your heart, if only for a second. Yet, it signals that the grace of Joy is once again active in your life.

Lord, let the grace of Joy flood into my heart and my soul.
Let me dwell in joyousness for its own sake, for the pure pleasure
of it. I do not need a reason or a purpose in order to feel joyful.
Perhaps thinking that way has kept joyfulness from my heart.
I have always put it within an equation, something I had to
earn or deserve. But the grace of Joy is pure, a sensation
unattached to reason—a pure mystical experience.

86

ANXIETY

Prayer

I HAD A GENUINE ANXIETY ATTACK last night, Lord. My
heart was pounding so rapidly I thought it would burst through
my chest. I don't have anxiety attacks. As I stared out the window
at 2:30 A.M., anxiety fogged my mind like humidity on a shower
door. Why was I feeling this way? Finally, I turned to You and
asked, "What is this? Is this some sort of emergency guidance?
What are You telling me? This is not the way I usually hear You
or sense Your guidance." I knew if I did not calm down, I would
begin to imagine things. I focused for who knows how long on
breathing myself into calmness, though I never became truly
calm. And then I was filled with images unlike anything I had ever
seen in my life: chaotic visions of all the upheavals happening—
and those yet to happen—due to climate change or some other
global crisis. The domino effect has begun. What have we done
to this Earth? We are living too big and want too much. And now
what? And now we pay the butcher's bill. I know the laws of healing, Lord. I know that a person cannot reverse choices already in
motion, but an individual can introduce new choices into his life
that influence the consequences of choices already made. We may
already be in debt, but we can influence that debt by not spending
more now—and by deciding to pay it down starting today. But
either way, we have to deal with it. We will not erase our climate
change debt. At the same time, the power we have to influence
the healing of the environment is extraordinary. Perhaps this is
the great spiritual challenge of our era, Lord. We must transcend
our differences, our boundaries, our languages, our religions, and
our politics and finally—finally—bond as one humanity. I fear our
capacity to make that choice, Lord. I really do. If anything is a test

of how conscious we believe ourselves to be, and how spiritual, this is that moment.

Guidance

We have all heard the warnings that we have 10 or 12 years to go before it's too late to reverse the impact of climate change. I have no idea how scientists decide on such figures. The shocking speed of the current glacier melt was not anticipated, for example. So who really knows how much time we have until these long predicted, catastrophic consequences arrive? Each year the summers are hotter and the winters are colder. The storms are more extreme and the floods are more widespread. We now have climate refugees, not just political ones. They can't all be turned away or imprisoned. Soon we won't be able to stop them. And if you were one of them, what would you do? No one anticipates becoming a refugee. They, too, thought it unimaginable until it happened to them. This is the era of the unthinkable. No other generations in recent memory have confronted climate change or environmental catastrophes such as we are facing. We are the ones who have to solve these predicaments. And they *are* predicaments, not problems or dilemmas. They do not have simple, easy solutions. They require that *we* change. Legislation will not force a glacier to stop melting. We need to change our lifestyles. Heaven will not step in and compensate for our refusal to make difficult choices. That is the law of healing applied to the whole. And this is a universe governed by laws and by prayer. Remember that prayer enhances the power of the laws. When enough prayers are said, generating enough grace, heaven intervenes and the natural laws yield to our needs. And that's what we call a miracle.

Grace

Lord, grant me the grace of Courage. I am alive now for a reason, and not just to collect things or to sit passively in a state of denial. I cannot tell myself that I am too old to be a participant in this great era of transformation, for why else am I here? You are speaking to all of us now, inspiring us to become allies of light and agents of life. We are in a birth canal, a passage between worlds. We are caterpillars becoming butterflies. But in that gelatinous state, we are so fragile. We are actively shedding one form and attempting to give birth to a new one. It is You who is calling us to give birth to that new form. That is the universal call now pulsing in our all souls. You are guiding us to succeed in this transition.

---

*Grant me the grace of Courage, Lord, that I may be
of service in this great cosmic hour of transformation.*

87

THE CALL *of* YOUR CHARISM

Prayer

LORD, I HAVE REFLECTED UPON the mystical concept of charism so many times. I know that charism is our "personal grace," the grace by which we are known to You. I absolutely love this description. I love that we each have a unique inner grace that is meant to be discovered and shared within our circle of life. I often think it's unfortunate that grace is invisible. How differently people would look upon heaven and prayer if grace could be seen. And if only one grace could be visible, perhaps the grace of charism would be the most seductive. For who would not turn inward in search of their own unique grace? Who would not begin a prayer life if they knew there was such inner treasure to be discovered? I think of each person's inner treasure as a shade of holy light that only *they* radiate, a light that embodies spiritual gifts perfectly calibrated to one's unique life path. Alas, such grace cannot be seen. Doubt remains potent. Still, the soul has a way of seducing people to seek that grace. People claim they were "born for something special." We hold being "ordinary" in contempt. We are enchanted with the idea of "discovering our highest potential." All of these are word salad for what we are genuinely seeking—our charism—but cannot name because we don't have the language. We each want contact with our charism, the grace bestowed upon us by You. That is the grace that prayer and faith release. I've come to realize, Lord, that without prayer, direct contact with grace is blinding. Perhaps there is great wisdom in the invisible movements of heaven and grace.

Guidance

We cannot stop seeking God. Regardless of what we call that search, we cannot stop ourselves from wanting to know the unique reason for our life. And it is a great suffering for us when we feel we may be wasting this gift of life. What you have been searching for is your charism, the grace by which God knows you. Within that grace is all that you are called to do—that which only you can do. That grace holds the seeds of all your potential, but it is your potential to love and to serve and to endure and to show compassion to others. Within your grace is your potential to channel grace to others. Each of us is born with a yearning to find our way to that grace. And with heaven's help, we usually do.

Grace

Take me down deep, Lord, and let me rest in holy listening so that I might recognize the grace of my Charism. Let me work through my reasons for asking until my reasons are pure. Beyond curiosity, beyond wonder, beyond boredom, beyond fear of "being ordinary." Help me ask in that humble way, because I am ready to let that grace change me.

Lord, I am ready to become an agent of grace in this world.

88

SLEEPWALKING *through* EVIL

Prayer

I HAVE TO ADMIT THAT I AM worried about the world, Lord, and that is a big worry. It's out of my league. I can only pray to You about this. People are sleepwalking through evil. They have become so accustomed to the behavior of the dark and the demonic that they hardly notice it, much less recognize it for what it is. So many people have dismissed the existence of evil, recoiling from the very word. Such arrogance is evil's greatest asset. Darkness relies upon human arrogance, greed, and weakness. These are the doorways through which evil can enter and have its way with us. People do not understand how evil operates. Or how good operates, for that matter. Angels, for example, have been commercialized and popularized. People have no problem believing in angels. They love that. They believe angels intervene to help them find parking spaces. But at least they *recognize* these celestial beings. They deny the dark angels, the demons who operate with equal latitude in this world. What forces do they think are there encouraging thoughts of suicide? What beings do they think are behind the scenes encouraging hatred and blame? The dark has never had such a hold on the global community, Lord. Even the Pope has warned that the Vatican is possessed by demons. Yet as a mystic, I understand this. Never before have so many people detached from prayer or from the belief that the soul requires the protection of grace—a truth that has been taught for thousands of years by mystics and spiritual leaders of all traditions. Only we of the nuclear age have dared to question the heavens. Paradoxically we have the most to lose. For what type of species celebrates the fact that it has created weapons capable of destroying itself? That is the ultimate victory of the dark. And we have given the dark its greatest tool: our arrogance.

Guidance

Evil is real. There is no discussion about this. I don't mince words. There are angels and there are demons. Arrogance and the need to reshape the reality of demons with endless vocabulary substitutes such as the word "negativity" are games. Evil is as active a force in our lives as divine guidance. And it is up to each person to take a deep breath, humble up, shift gears, and make the decision to reboot a clear and conscious connection to their conscience, their active, organic divine guidance system. No one is conscious enough to regulate or monitor themselves. We must rely on the intuitive guidance we receive from our soul. This intuitive guidance—our conscience—alerts us to what is right and wrong, good and evil, humane and unjust, moral and immoral. These codes of the soul are trans-religious. They are universal. They are inherent sacred knowledge woven into the wiring of our intuition. And this mystical knowledge is meant to govern our relationship to the light and the dark. That we have this relationship between light and darkness explains why free will and choice are so powerful. At the end of the day, every choice we make either enhances the light or feeds the dark. That's how the system of creation works. It's all about choice and consequence, action and reaction. Our decisions direct the creation and influence of all the experiences we have in our personal and global life. Yes, life is as organized—and simple—as that.

Grace

Pride and arrogance feed our desire to control our world and everything and everyone in it. We think we know what's best—for *us*. That attitude comes from a blend of fear, common sense, experience, and the mother lode of all fears: the loss of control.

The grace we need when we find ourselves spinning out of control is Humility. Nothing short of a sense of our own *insignificance* can snap us out of an attack of self-importance.

Lord, grant me the grace of Humility. Keep me from the temptation to redesign this Universe according to my needs. Who am I to decide how this cosmos is designed? Do I know how many planets and stars there are? Do I know what happens after I die, or who I was before I was born? How do I know what forces govern this brief life I have? All the great mystics have told us that this world has two forces that are always falling in and out of balance. I can feel those forces active within me. I know the truth of that teaching. And I know how I create imbalance within myself: I make dark choices. I know from experience that darkness has ~ authority. I feel it in my blood and bones. Therefore, Lord, grant me the grace to see clearly. And keep me under the grace of protection, Lord. Lead me not into temptation but into and ever toward the light.

89

THE POWER *of* MIRACULOUS LOVE

Prayer

I TOOK A LONG WALK WITH YOU this morning, Lord, and contemplated the power of love in the midst of violence—around us and within us. Love has endless expressions. It's personal, impersonal, cosmic, sacred, and holy. It's all those forces and so much more. Love is that mysterious thread from the heart that binds us to someone no matter where they are. Even after they've returned home to You. Love never evaporates. I love my family members who have passed as much as if they were still with me. Time, space, and the transition of life make no difference. And yet, do we really trust the power of love? I'm not certain that we do. Perhaps in small ways, but these are the times that call for *miraculous* love—the real thing. We need to love, big time and with no exceptions. We need to love with our hearts on the line. We need to crack open and discover what and who we are capable of loving in this time of chaos. Ultimately, that choice comes down to trusting You, Lord. And perhaps this extreme time of social unrest will activate in us a power of collective love unlike anything we have experienced before. A love of humanity, a love of our planet, a love of all living creatures. That is the quality of love these times call for. Tsunamis of love can transform everything. I believe that. I believe we can heal the wounds of the past and the ongoing horrors occurring each day in front of our eyes. You will not do this work for us. You will not save us from our fear of discovering the power of love. I know that. Maybe the first miracle we need to experience is to break through our own fear of loving without borders.

Guidance

Everything about what it means to be a human being is getting tested right now. And I mean everything: from what we believe to be true about the nature of God to our values and ethics to whether we believe our climate is changing to how to proceed into the future—with or without weapons of mass destruction. Even the concept of "mass destruction" takes my breath away. What kind of people specialize in "mass destruction" and then go home at night and eat dinner? And when will we stop believing that killing others is the way to keep us safe? It's never worked. We are more paranoid and frightened and contaminated as a society than we have ever been. We believe in destruction as protection—and have stopped believing in the protection of grace and divine guidance. This trade has cost us our collective soul. A population does not see the level of decay in mental and emotional health around us because it is thriving on its belief system. We are not thriving; we are spiritually starving. As a society we are on a respirator when it comes to integrity, morals, and ethics. We are incapable of problem solving because we lack the integrity to actually *admit* the problems we face. We have grown so accustomed to hearing lies that we are not even aware how sinful those lies are to our soul. And conscious lies *are* sins. Sin is the correct word, drawn directly out of the holy language vocabulary. Deliberate deception is a sin. It's not a mistake, it's not a boo-boo, it's not a misstep. When the intent of the speaker is to deceive the listener—while engaging their trust—a sin has been committed. Forgetting this, we have become a society whose only resources are blame, hatred, and spin. This is cowardice, which is yet another consequence of deception. It will take a miracle of love, a cosmic-sized infusion of holy, mystical light, to raise the bar of our consciousness. We must lift our blinders in order to once again see our fellow human beings. We come from traditions of creativity, enterprise, independence, vitality, generosity, vision, and plenty-to-go-around. We are not selfish, afraid of loss, afraid to share, afraid of not having enough. We do not talk like that. I did not grow up thinking like

that. Creativity is a mindset, a way of thinking, and a way of praying. Today we have the opportunity to discover what love can do.
We must respond to that opportunity. It won't be easy, I know. I have
to work at it constantly myself. I pray all the time for the strength
to hold up my end of the commitment to be loving when so much
tempts me toward judgment. But all of our lives depend on it.

Grace

Lord, Your grace of miraculous Love is greater than any love
I can know on my own. I know personal love, but that is small
love—like a grain of sand on the beach. Miraculous Love is the
ocean itself, capable of reshaping the shoreline, keeping all the
ships afloat and sustaining life endlessly. You sent us the message
to be the hands and heart and servants of heaven in the world, to
be the physical presence of divine truth. Nothing is more difficult,
Lord, and nothing is more essential.

---

*Lord, tie my heart to a thread of miraculous Love, and watch
over me always. Help me be a channel for this love through my
thoughts and actions, my words and the content of my heart.*

90

GUIDANCE ON SUICIDE

Prayer

I SPEAK TO YOU AS IF YOU WALK every step of my life with me, Lord, because I believe You do. And I've grown accustomed to these deep, reflective, meditative conversations with You. I can sense Your special grace in moments of holy listening. It tells me that a sacred portal is present. And so, now I turn to You for counsel on suicide. What do I say to someone who has attempted suicide—and might not be done with trying? And what kind of counsel can be offered to friends and family members who have lost someone to suicide? And why, Lord, is the choice to end one's life—this drastic option for coping with pain—so common these days? I need Your grace-filled guidance and counsel as I sit here this morning, pen in hand, resting in holy listening. The hours have passed today in quietude. Little by little, thoughts have melted into the soil of my soul, like soft raindrops. We suffer for many reasons. I know that. There is no shortage of good reasons why we struggle in life. But the absence of the grace of hope can make our suffering unendurable. What is it a person should hope for when a situation seems unresolvable or unending? Is the answer hidden within the mystery of the power of acceptance? In life, some obstacles must be accepted as assignments while remaining unexplained. That is all there is to it. The inability to accept and endure a difficult stage, challenge, change, illness, or consequence can lead us to lose hope, Lord. The absence of hope, given enough time, inevitably leads us to a breaking point. We are creatures that need the grace of hope in order to endure what we think is unendurable. We need it as much as we require oxygen; indeed, grace is the oxygen of the soul. I know that prayer is the generator of grace. I recognize the presence of the graces of endurance and hope in me now, Lord, because they animate thoughts within me that sustain me, regardless of my circumstances. You work in such mysterious ways, Lord. It only takes one prayer for heaven to show up. People have told me that someone showed up out of the clear blue when they were at their lowest point and helped them back to life. Others shared stories of reading the right book when they hardly had the strength to read anymore, or watching an interview on a program they ordinarily would not watch. And yet, it was just what they needed to hear. You always show up. It only takes one small prayer and the slightest amount of faith. Lord, please send the graces of hope and endurance to the many who find themselves at the breaking point. Surround them with the stamina to live one more day—and sometimes just one more hour. Send healing angels to assist them through this dark passage, no matter how long, no matter how dark.

Guidance

Suicide is on the rise for many reasons. Including hopelessness, which is the absence of faith that anything can or will change. Rarely is it mentioned that hope and faith are graces and that prayer is the engine of grace. Rarely. Heaven does indeed work in mysterious ways, none of which are like us humans. That fact is often disappointing to people—and has caused some to question the existence of the holy domain altogether. To this my response is "How has such skepticism been good for your health and well-being?" Our energetic nature sparkles only when it is being nourished by the graces. For is it really possible to be emotionally happy without hope? Or calm and centered in a relationship without inner trust? Or emotionally strong and steady in life—and relationships—without the grace of endurance? Nope. Grace is required. It is soul oxygen. Like oxygen, heaven is invisible, silent, and humble in its maneuverings—but essential to our wellness. Heaven does not consider what is best for our ego first but what is best for our *soul*. This truth may not often satisfy us in the immediacy of our desires. But looking back we discover that heaven's guidance has been woven into the design of our life, every step of the way.

Grace

Lord, grant me and others in need an abundance of Hope and Endurance, especially in the times of my life when nothing makes sense and I feel I am at my breaking point. That fear is like none other. It is terrifying not to know what to do, or whom to go to for help. I need to count on You to be that source of help, especially when I am tumbling backward.

Grant me Your protection, Lord, now and always.

91

THE WAY of the HEART

Prayer

MY PRAYER TODAY, LORD, is to refine my awareness of the needs of others in my life. I may not be able to respond to everyone with words or actions, but I can respond with prayer and grace. I know when I am inadvertently sensing the energy field of another person. I have become a finely tuned instrument now. What I did not anticipate years ago when I followed the call to do intuitive readings was that all inner roads inevitably lead to love. It's not personal love that I feel. In fact, Lord, You have given me the grace of an impersonal heart, something that would have terrified me as a young woman. But I have learned with utter amazement that there is nothing but room in this heart. Some people have slipped in who never would have gotten into that smaller heart of mine— ever. Funny, that. Love is an astonishing force. It never runs out. And love doesn't require a person. I can just dwell on love and it starts flowing. I don't know where or to whom, but the sensation is utterly extraordinary. Love is a mighty force. Perhaps it is the name we have given to Your light.

Guidance

We learn early that we cannot control love. Love controls us. It can possess us. Love gives us the stamina to take care of people we love, sometimes for decades—simply because we love them. Love calls us to forgive, and to be patient, and to endure, and to have compassion. Love often demands more of us than we think we can give—only to discover we *can* give that much (and more) if we have to. There are people we wish we could stop loving. Life would be easier if only we could stop loving them. And there are people we wish we could love more. Love has a mind of its own. And then there is the wish that we could be loved more by certain others. We cannot make others love us; and we ourselves can only love those we do. That's the way of personal love. But beyond personal love is something else: impersonal, universal love. Love as love. Love itself. It's the difference between the personal light bulb in your room, which does provide some light, and the sun—which is light itself. One is personal and the other belongs to no one. It just is. That type of love blasts the walls off your personal heart, and you feel love—sunlight—for no particular reason at all. You don't need to love a particular person in order to know love. You don't have to have a target, a purpose, a "special someone" to know what love—or light—is. You know because you are standing in the direct path of the sun. You feel it. You know it. And that's when you know love is the light that all living creatures crave the most.

Grace

For all the many ways we think about Love, rarely do we refer to it as a grace. Rarely do we pray to be given the grace, the inner stamina, to allow the power of Love to come through us. To let it flow, unobstructed by our fear of its power to elevate, liberate, heal, and transform other people. Our fear of the transforming power of Love should stand as proof of how powerful every grace is in our lives.

Lord, thank you for the grace of Love. It is a curious grace,
in that I have often felt great pain in my heart as well as great joy
from its power. I realize now that I am glimpsing the unnecessary pain
we generate in our lives because we do not choose Love. It is not
You who makes us suffer. Maybe if we can Love enough,
our fear of each other will diminish.

92

SERVICE *and* SACRIFICE

Prayer

LORD, I SEE THAT YOU ARE drafting a new type of saint
and martyr into action these days. This virus is spreading like a
forest fire, and thousands of human beings—healers and true servants of humanity—have heeded the call to serve with their skills
and their lives. Many are falling ill now from the very crisis they
are battling. Is this not the way of war? Many of us who are not
these healers are watching this with tears in our eyes, pain in our
hearts, and rage at how much more we could be doing—but aren't.
It is so easy to speak of being of service. But service at a soul level
is never really a personal choice, is it? I imagine so many of these
health care workers are breaking in two, knowing that they might
be putting their families at risk—and perhaps already have. Service of the soul has always demanded sacrifice. Maybe soul service
and sacrifice are woven together in some way, Lord. Perhaps what
seems like a sacrifice at the time is really the release of something
that would become an unbearable burden to us much later in our
lives. Who knows how Your wisdom works. I only know that in
some way, caring for others is never the wrong choice.

Guidance

Sometimes soul service requires the ultimate sacrifice, as we
are now witnessing from so many. We've seen it during times of
war. But we are fighting psychic wars now. We are on energetic
battlefields. We must all see ourselves as living not *on* the battlefield but *within* the battlefield. We are the living, breathing battlefields for the virus. How else would we learn that we co-create this
reality of ours?

Grace

At times like this, each of us needs to ask for the graces of Healing, Compassion, Strength, and Courage. We must pour these graces out to every person risking their life in order to protect the rest of us who have the luxury of staying in our homes for the majority of the hours of the day. And even when this crisis is over—and eventually it will be—there will be others to come. We must never, ever forget to keep in our prayers those who are called into soul service and sacrifice: health care professionals, grocery store clerks, municipal workers, postal workers, and every public employee serving their community.

Lord, protect those You have called into the service of others. Please keep them—and their families—safe from harm. I feel so much love for these people. My heart is filled with so much gratitude. The only way I can think to share that love is to pray for their well-being. So I ask You to shine Your holy light upon all of them, and the many in need of Your mercy whom they serve.

93

HELP ME MAKE *the* COURAGEOUS CHOICE

Prayer

THERE ARE RIGHT CHOICES, LORD, and there are wrong choices. The difference is pretty obvious to me these days. And then there are courageous choices—the ones that bubble up from my gut. In fact, one is bubbling now. And I don't like it, not at all. I don't like it because I know it's the right thing to do . . . it is what I *have* to do, but I don't *want* to do it. I need that type of courage that is beyond ordinary courage. I need the grace of courage. I need Your intervention to surround this choice, to breathe grace into the words I choose and to bless the consequences of those words. Sometimes that laser-like clarity of mine is difficult to live with. This is one of those times. I never mind turning that skill on myself; with myself I am ruthless. But there are times when I know I need to be similarly ruthless with someone else. And what needs to be said feels like a burden. It makes me wonder how often those close to me have felt that way about wanting to say something delicate to me. Perhaps all the time. We need holy witnesses in our lives: those who love us enough to tell us the truth. Those we trust deeply enough to listen to when they reflect that we are straying from our path or our integrity. We cannot always see ourselves clearly. Holy witnesses are blessings in our lives, even though at times the messages they bring can sting like cosmic-sized bees. These people are rare souls in our lives, Lord. That, I have come to know. And today I must be a holy witness to someone I love dearly. And that is also the reason I find myself so hesitant to speak up. I want to ask You to reveal what cannot be revealed: to show me, in advance, the consequences of the conversation I know I must have. I know those moments are not yet determined, and yet I also know that You already know how it will go. Both are true in that mystical way in which contradictions that exist in our human world blend together as one in the holy realm.

Guidance

Truth organizes events and conversations. The power and electricity of the truth generates sparks in our inner atmosphere, making us feel as if we will explode unless we say what we are feeling or thinking. We must let the truth come out—or we will indeed erupt. And we must be willing to hear truth spoken to us. And of equal importance, we must learn *how* to share truth—how to remember that "our truth" is only partial. For none of us really sees the other that clearly, that fully, that deeply. We know each other in tiny fragments, as others know us. And those fragments are always shifting, with every new insight or positive action we take. So when we need to share an insight with another, let us always keep in mind how little we really know about that person—about the depth of their soul. Let us remember that we are viewing that individual through our eyes, not divine eyes.

Grace

We need, in fact we *require*, the grace of Courage to examine the truth within ourselves and in others. Truth is the greatest change agent in life. We need Courage to see the truth, to accept the truth in ourselves first, or we will not be clear-sighted or honest about our motivations in speaking with others.

*Grant me the grace of Courage, Lord, when I know what
needs to be said but am afraid to say it. Be with me in these
moments of choice, when there really is no choice but to speak the
truth. I know when You are guiding me. What is more foolish than to
seek guidance—and then pretend not to hear it? Having the Courage
to act on that guidance requires yet another grace: Trust. One choice
leads to another, and yet another. And so, the wheel of life turns. No
wonder the mystics wrote in so many different ways, "Keep God close."
Life is indeed a labyrinth, a journey of endless turns that can appear
at times to lead us nowhere. But ultimately, we arrive at You.*

94

THE PORTAL *of* LOVE

Prayer

PEOPLE ASK ME ALL THE TIME, LORD, how to pray. They ask who I am praying to and how I know "anyone" is out there. (They're talking about You, Lord.) They want to know how I know I am not just talking to myself. I tell them that those are logical questions. After all, I am known to talk to myself quite frequently. Yet I never feel that flow of grace when I talk to myself that I feel talking to You. How I wish I could transfer the experience of grace to the person asking me those questions. I compare it to what love feels like. I tell them to focus on all the love they feel for someone, to drench themselves in that love for a second. And then I tell them to imagine that I have no idea what love feels like, and I ask them to describe the feeling to me. Once they have, I ask, "How do I know love is real if I have no experience of it myself? Yet I am drawn to seek it out. Even the idea of love is seductive to me. There must be something to this thing called love, for all of you can't be crazy. All of you can't be imagining this invisible force that bonds you so tightly to another person. But you can't prove to me that it exists, not scientifically at least. You can't show it to me, measure it, or put it in a box. Yet, that invisible substance controls everything within you. That is the degree to which I know the holy realm is real. It is as real and powerful and present to me as love is to you." Lord, I think that love is a portal to the holy realm, a way to You. Love often doesn't make sense. People do harm, but still we love them. I have so often listened to people tell me they are afraid to love. How can that be? How can a human being be afraid to open wide the doors and windows of their heart? Instead a person should say, "Hmm, I wonder how big and wide and deep my heart is. I wonder how my life would change—how *I* would change—if

I just let love have its way with me." Love is the fuel of miracles. Love sustains us through the most difficult times. I waited too long to learn that, Lord. It's mystical currency. It's the one force that scares the dark the most. Love is Your light in action.

Guidance

I've heard people say they are afraid to love because they might get hurt. I say, get hurt and get it over with! And then keep going. Those songs about mending a broken heart are utter nonsense. A heart is meant to be broken—*broken wide open*. You do not "mend" a broken heart. You fill in those places with people—and lots of them. Small, closed hearts are nothing but trouble. They generate small, closed thoughts. You love in small, insecure ways. Instead, love big. Love wild. And imagine love way beyond romantic fantasies. Love is most powerful when you know it as a cosmic, impersonal, divine force—unattached to a person or a reason. Love just as love. It comes through as kindness, compassion, patience, service, generosity, and forgiveness, and not just toward those you know but to everyone.

Grace

Divine Love is the grace you need in order to heal the wounds in your heart that you cannot heal yourself. All of us know what it is like to be hurt so badly that we can hardly breathe. We may want to forgive that person, and perhaps that individual wants to forgive us, but we are at a complete dead end. The love we once felt is frozen, if not completely drained from our system. Divine Love is the grace that revitalizes and renews our capacity to love again. It provides you with the strength to forgive that which you thought you could never forgive, and to get on with friendships or partnerships that you are better with than without.

Lord, every time I stand in the sunlight, let me be reminded of holy, divine light and the power of Love, especially when I am not feeling loving. In those moments, let Your Love shine upon me, that I may live that day as a channel of Love for others. At the very least, prevent me from harming others—from passing to them any anger or personal suffering I might be feeling that day. Those issues are mine to heal. So, lead me through the portal of Love, one day at a time. And hover over me, Lord, on this holy journey.

95

COSMIC-SIZED *Love*

Prayer

WE ARE NOT ABLE TO LOVE, cosmic sized, without an invitation from You. I finally understood this, Lord, after years and years of studying the lives of the mystics and saints. They had cosmic-sized hearts. They also shared something else—a direct invitation from heaven to be channels for the power of that love and the consequences of that power during their lifetime. For years I wondered why all those saints suffered so much, why they lived such bizarre, extreme lives after their encounters with the holy realm. *Had they been driven mad?* I wondered. I did not want to be interested in such things, Lord—but I was. I was captivated. Why were they so impassioned, so devoted? How did they describe both states of ecstasy *and* deep suffering? Sometimes, Lord, I believe You answer us slowly, gradually, through a long inner unfolding of understanding. Or maybe it's simply that I could not comprehend the answer all at once. But I have finally grasped, at least in small part, that holy knowledge. And truth often generates in us the response of the agony and the ecstasy, the falling away of the scales of illusion while realizing we are still imprisoned by them. I see the pain in people who know climate change is real, for example. They realize nature is conscious and alive, and they have to cope with those who deny this knowledge. The pain is visceral. Yet as they answer the inner call to act on behalf of nature, they know an ecstasy as well: they understand what it means to serve life for life's sake. That is cosmic-sized love, and it demands sacrifice. Teresa of Ávila described the soul as a diamond with seven mansions but notes that she herself waited 20 years to be called to the fourth mansion of the soul. She waited for You to invite her into the sacred cosmic heart. Because without Your invitation, love that powerful would have crushed her small human heart. If we are to channel cosmic love, we cannot waste our time with small, petty nonsense. The smallness of our ego has to be cleaned up. Which is no small task, Lord. But compared to cosmic, holy love and its healing authority, healing the self is so worth the effort. And how difficult can the task really be, with Your help? As Teresa of Ávila taught her nuns, "With God, nothing is impossible."

Guidance

I believe the grace of Healing can dissolve any harm—even the grip of the most painful memory. Though the memory may remain, it no longer has its claws in our heart; it no longer "hunts us down" during the night. I've learned that healing requires surrendering into the power of grace, like falling backward into the arms of a trusted friend you know will catch you. Ironically, you cannot turn around to check whether they are there because then you risk losing your balance and falling sideways. You have to fall back with complete trust. Likewise, when you pray for healing—of anything—you have to surrender not just the wound but *who* you are and *how* you are. You can't hold on to the inner vision of yourself as still needing to be angry at someone. Not even just a bit; it's all or nothing. And that degree of surrender is extremely difficult. I won't kid you. It is an ego death. You can't do this without prayer and grace.

Grace

We can call ourselves healers, but without the grace of Healing, we are cars without fuel. The grace of Healing comes from the Divine. We channel it to those in need. But we ourselves need to be prepared to serve as channels for this grace; thus the story of the wounded healer. First the grace, like a fragrant cologne, is given to us to heal ourselves. And then when we are clear enough, it flows through us like potent perfume to heal others.

Lord, please let the grace of Healing pour down upon me like holy rain, especially when I am unaware that I am in need of it. Let the grace of Healing flow through my mind, my heart, and my soul at all times, preventing darkness from finding a place to incubate in my system. Help me heal the first negative thought so I do not have time to create a second one. And let the grace of Healing flow from me to others, Lord, in any and all ways that it can.

96

TIME *to* HUMBLE UP

Prayer

I HAVE TO ADMIT THAT TONIGHT I am in deep despair, Lord. I have heard far too many people say that they are "sending thoughts and prayers" to those who have just experienced horrific crises in our society. But they are not actually praying, Lord. They are saying those words because they are afraid to tell the truth. They are hiding behind holy language, using it as a political shield. Perhaps some *have* said prayers for those who are victims of violence; only You would know that. But I know how profound and real the power of prayer is, and I know that to say you are going to pray for someone and fail in that commitment is a soul violation. Prayer is not politics. I get that I am having a tantrum right now, Lord. I am; I own it. But if people truly believed in You, they would not dare to speak of prayer—of invoking Your assistance—without acknowledging they are on sacred ground. But someday those people themselves will need Your help. They will need the power of grace to come into their lives. And I know You will answer those prayers too. You always do. Good thing You don't take my advice! (I have noticed through the years that You never have asked for my advice. This business of guidance is a one-way street.) So I will humble up. I will get back to my seat in the theater, so to speak. Who am I to have a cosmic fit? I have no idea who has which divine assignment down here. I can't get over how I still have to remind myself of truths I've known for decades now. I think about Buddha's teaching that life is full of illusions . . . that I know better, that other people should do this or that. But with Your help I have made *some* progress, Lord. I can feel that wretched twitch in my gut that tells me I am out of line. That it's time to humble up. The twitch that reminds me—yet again—that You are not here to

251

serve me, but I to serve You. Alrighty then. We're done here, Lord. Back to my chair in the theater.

Guidance

What is easier than to decide that you know what's going on and that you have the right answer? Or that your side is the "right" side? And how often have you later discovered that you actually had no idea what you were talking about—or worse, that you were dead wrong? Then you promise yourself you will not make that error in judgment again. You will not fall into the trap of overreacting or deciding that you know better. And then . . . and then . . . well, you know the drill. Spiritual teachings do not emphasize the need for humility to grind us into the ground—to "humiliate" us—but to prevent us, ironically, from humiliating ourselves through our own arrogance.

Grace

Humility is protection against our own worst instincts, among them our tendency to judge situations and people we know nothing about. How much can we know, anyway? We can hardly figure out what *we* are up to half the time, much less what strangers are doing. Even family members and friends have their personal reasons—and dare I say, inner guidance—that we know nothing about. Again and again I have learned that we each have a seat in the theater of life from which we view the world, and it's best to remember that we have no idea what the view looks like from any other seat.

Lord, grant me the grace of Humility. I will remind myself to "humble up," especially when that judgmental part of me gets going. You have saved me from my own worst instincts more than once. When I've been flooded with negative thoughts about someone, I have suddenly experienced an instantaneous burst of compassion for that same person—reminding me that I was out of line. I know the power of this grace because I need it so often. So, hover over me, Lord, with Humility—a grace I wish I didn't need as much as I do.

97

WATCH OVER US, LORD

Prayer

LORD, KEEP WATCH OVER US. Every one of us. I know You are watching this world. You watched over the world wars while they happened, but that didn't stop them from happening. We cannot understand the reasons why things happen as they do or exactly how we influence the greater events of our lives. But we do influence them. We *are* agents of creation. We just do not realize that we have such authority and thus we are misusing it. For example, our biggest obstacle, Lord, is that we can't figure out how to work together as one humanity. That would resolve a great many of these crises within a few years. Just like that. That's what we need, Lord. We need You to watch over us, preventing us from acting on our worst instincts, especially now when we are facing a global health crisis. Can we rise to the power of love and the realization that what we do to one person, we are doing to ourselves? We are one huge, cosmic-sized, living, holy body of life. It's so obvious why we keep sabotaging love: we fear sharing what we have. We fear giving up the power of greed. I get that. But now that we are confronted with the choice between global demise and global transformation, who would not choose to release the power of love? I have to say, Lord, that it really baffles me. Can hatred and fear really be so great that a person would choose weapons over life? I guess so because we are looking at it every day. But I know that all things can shift in the blink of an eye, as the Buddha taught. All it takes are the right words—the holy language—to penetrate enough people. I know it. I believe it. Watch over us, Lord. All the living creatures I see all the time are pulling for life.

Guidance

What will it take to get us to change? How many more crises do we need before we get the message that we are one humanity—that we are the same as people everywhere? Greed is poison. No one leaves this planet with their bank account. All the riches in the world will not buy you one more moment of life.

Grace

To have an Epiphany is to experience a sudden awakening to another more vibrant—indeed mystical—level of consciousness. Such an experience is given to a person. You cannot initiate an Epiphany. It is an act of grace. You emerge a different human being, destined to a different life than the one you were living a second before. The astronaut Edgar Mitchell had such an Epiphany from his spacecraft. He was looking at Earth from afar and realized that he could not see the borders of any nation. All he could see was this beautiful blue planet—home to all of us. An Epiphany is a mystical experience that ignites a new life path in a person, a download of grace that generates an entirely new understanding of the world.

Lord, there is so much I do not understand, that I am incapable of understanding. But if I am ready and able to see more, to comprehend more, then open the eyes of my soul. Grant me the grace of an Epiphany, so that I may absorb more truth and understand the divine code of life ever more deeply, each day.

98

LIGHT in the DARK NIGHT

Prayer

BE MY LIGHT IN THE DARK, Lord, my candle at night. For that is when shadows—Teresa's reptiles—start dancing on the walls of my mind. Somehow these demons still manage to get in. I think I am past the stage of small fears, only to discover I am not. And that enrages me! I expect more from my faith in You by now. But this fear is not from lack of belief or trust in You, Lord. No, it is from my fear of what people are capable of doing when they are frightened—perhaps myself most of all. I do not fear *You*. Hardly. It is the outside world that makes me tremble. To me, You are the known, the trusted, that which has been consistent in my life. This world, on the other hand, is everything unknown and capricious. It is filled with psychic free radicals igniting bad thoughts in people's minds like firecrackers. I need Your light to hold me steady, especially when my own sense of "what might happen" takes hold of my thoughts. I ask You, Lord, to lift me above those thought forms. Drench me in your grace of quietude, which can make even the darkest moments feel like a distant memory.

Guidance

Teresa of Ávila was right when she described negative thoughts, attitudes, and emotions as reptiles creeping into our minds and hearts. They are invaders, and they do see better at night than we do. We may think we have overcome a fear, a negative influence, or a pattern of control—only to discover that it has found a different way in. It makes its way through the lesser-known passages of our unconscious, and once again we are in the gravity field of a Buddha-sized illusion. We tumble toward the dark side, falling down that long interior tunnel. Our worst nightmares wake from their slumber as we whirl by their emotional cubby holes. *Ugh*, we think, as we realize we have awakened our dragons, our gargoyles, and our ghosts. And once again we brace ourselves for a haunting. Just when we thought we had cleansed ourselves of these unwelcomed psychic homesteaders, we are reminded that they actually own some of our inner real estate. They are not just passing through. We must make peace with them, one way or another. We have to allow them to stay because they are ours. They are *our* dragons, *our* gargoyles, and *our* ghosts. But we can remember they stay on our terms; they must follow our rules. And that negotiation requires prayer. Ordinary thoughts and words do not have the authority to challenge darkness. We can calm ourselves with ordinary words; we can tell ourselves that things will be fine and there is nothing to be afraid of. But without grace, words can only calm us for a brief period of time. Light, on the other hand, has authority over the dark. Words animated by grace penetrate into your soul, shattering negative thoughts and replacing them with holy messages. *You'll be fine*, they remind you. *Things will work out.* Transmissions of grace have the immediate effect of resetting your entire being. People have often told me they heard a voice tell them they would be fine, and they knew it was true. It never occurred to them to question whether they really heard that voice. They knew they had, and they immediately trusted that holy messenger.

Grace

The precious grace of holy Listening settles deeply into us, calming our inner being and penetrating every cell in our bodies. The Divine is organic, just like us. Divine light flows through our blood and bones, through our thoughts and emotions. That is the presence of God in us. Don't listen for words . . . feel and sense your way into holiness.

I ask for the grace of holy Listening, Lord, when I need to enter into silence. Help me quiet my inner reptiles so I can listen for that stillness that is You—my eternal candle in the night. I need that grace more than I realize. So often I can let my guard down, and suddenly the size of the world and its problems appear overwhelming. We cannot risk thinking that they are overwhelming and insurmountable, Lord. With You, all things are possible, even finding ways through the darkest passages in our lives.

99

While WE SLEEP

Prayer

WATCH OVER THIS WORLD while we sleep, Lord. Send Your messengers of light to whisper to us in our dreams. Give us hope as we wake up to each new day of our life. It is a blessing to be embraced by the morning, knowing that the new day holds great possibilities. That thought alone is a blessing: a holy spark of grace that has the power to ignite enthusiasm for everything about my life. It takes so little grace to help us see our life anew. Just a little bit of hope, fortitude, or love can breathe life into even the most depleted soul. And we do get exhausted, Lord. Sometimes ordinary rest is not enough to replenish our bodies, minds, and souls. All of us could use those holy night messengers who deliver comfort and grace, who gently take us to the healing realm and illuminate our souls with healing grace while we sleep through the night. Wrap this world in Your care, Lord, now more than ever. It is fractured with darkness and fear, and so many wonder if the heavens are vacant. For those of us who know better, we will keep watch down here with prayers for all—as You keep watch over all of us while we sleep.

Guidance

I remember a story of a woman—a journalist—who returned to the Catholic Church after years of absence. Her family happened to be out of town over Christmas, and she wanted to be anything but alone that Christmas Eve. So she wandered into the first church she could find. As it happened, it was a church devoted to the Franciscans and the Poor Clares. (The Poor Clares are the cloistered community of nuns associated with Saint Francis of

Assisi, the founder of the Franciscans.) When the time came for the Franciscan priest to offer communion to the few parishioners gathered there, he first approached a small wooden screen built into the wall by the side of the altar. Sliding it open, he delivered communion to nuns living "behind those walls." Her curiosity got the best of her, so she remained after Mass to ask the priest about what she had witnessed. He told her about the Poor Clares. She could not fathom that these women had chosen to live such cloistered lives. One of them, the priest told her, had not left the building for 68 years. She inquired, "What are they doing in there? I mean, what can they possibly be doing for sixty-eight years in this building?" The priest responded, "They are praying." Still curious—as well as frustrated—she asked, "Who are they praying for?" The priest, looking her directly in the eyes, replied, "For you." These cloistered nuns, he explained, are devoted to praying for all those who do not pray for themselves. They are praying on behalf of those who do not realize they need prayers to help them through their trials and difficulties. They pray for the world, to be channels of grace for all humanity. I treasure this story as a reminder that there are many ways to be of service and to give to this world. Prayer is one of them. It doesn't matter that you cannot see the good it does, or the grace you generate when you do it. You can't see it any more than you can see the grace that is bestowed upon you when you ask for help or guidance. But all of us have experienced the results of grace in our lives. Holy language, when spoken in the privacy of your heart as a prayer or a thought and sent to another, is a transmission of grace.

Grace

The grace of Awareness heightens your senses to your world and to those who dwell within it. It allows you to become ever more aware of others—to notice their fragileness, how they are aging, what they are looking for, what makes them happy or sad. Instead of wanting to be noticed, the more wondrous task is to notice others. Very few people get up in the morning and have a list of people they want to avoid and ignore that day. And yet too few of us make the conscious effort to *notice*. So look upon others with wonder, as if they were living storybooks—because every person is exactly that. And then listen to their stories. In the end, we grow in the Awareness that we share so much of the same experience with others. We have never, ever been alone.

Lord, grant me the grace of Awareness. Keep me ever growing in my Awareness that I am one with all humanity; that what I do to one, I do to all; that as it is in heaven, so it is on Earth; that every thought and feeling I have is also a choice, and that choice is an act of creation; and that all life breathes together. You are watching over all creation even while we sleep, but we, too, must be the caretakers of life with every conscious choice we make.

100

Choose LOVE, *Whatever* YOU DO

Prayer

WATCH OVER THOSE I LOVE, LORD—my family and friends and all the many people who have contributed so much to my life in ways they will never, ever realize. We love in so many different ways. Love has so many expressions, really. I have such deep love for my family and friends. I know them so well, and perhaps love them all the more because they know my quirks and vulnerabilities and still love me. That's obvious love, and effortless. But through the years, Lord, You have blessed me with the grace of loving people in ways I did not expect. Or perhaps this feeling is a hybrid of love, gratitude, and awe, all mixed together. It is a heart sensation that now dwells in me as if it were always present. I am so mindful of the blessing of sharing my life with so many and the gift of being able to help them with their life challenges. I would never have sought a path of helping people, Lord. I still laugh about that. I wanted to be a writer so I could work alone and not have to be with people. But then, how would I have learned anything at all? How would I have discovered the nature of love, the soul, the power of prayer, and You? You make me laugh . . . really. Thank You for showing me that this life is all about love.

Guidance

Whatever you do, do it with love. If you can't feel love in your heart, then go for kindness, respect, patience—or stay silent. As difficult as it is to comprehend—and I grant you, it is difficult if not impossible to believe—absolutely everything in our lives is a stage set up for love. The Buddha knew it. Jesus taught it. They

were not delusional. We just find the holy challenge of unconditional love to be overwhelming. And it *is* overwhelming. Soul
love requires the help of grace. We all find ourselves in settings in
which we are called—and I do mean *called*—to channel grace. We
are not in such a situation for personal reasons, or to receive love.
We are there *to radiate love itself*—the grace of love. Most people
are not able to handle that type of assignment because it's a task
that is entirely about serving others. Most people want to know
"What's in this for me?" and "How are people feeling about me?"
It's inconceivable that you could be sent into a relationship, or a
job, or an organization just to be a lightning rod of grace. But such
assignments are given—and not infrequently. Nelson Mandela
had such an assignment, for example, as did Gandhi. (Mind you, I
need to mention well-known people as examples. Countless other
people are called to such assignments, but we do not know them.)
No matter who is called or what the assignment looks like, at the
end of the day, it's always about one choice: love.

Grace

You know the grace of Love is powerful stuff. Just keep in
mind that Love is a grace that is meant to be shared. You can't run
out of Love. So share it, "waste" it, pour it out in thoughts, words,
and actions. Think Love. Speak Love. Become Love. Breathe in
this grace 24/7.

The grace of Love is pure bliss. It doesn't have a downside, Lord.
That grace only inspires us and makes us want to do the impossible
for the people we Love. No wonder we associate You with Love.
We turn to You when we need the impossible to happen in our lives.
Love seems to be the way to reach You, the phone line You answer
most directly. When we combine Love with faith, we get right through
to You. I cannot ask for the grace of Love without being willing to share
that grace—I know that. But I have also learned that this is a grace
that won't stay put in a person's heart. It longs to be shared
and it has Your imprint on it. The wonder of it all . . .

A Final Thought

I KNOW THAT HAVING FAITH AND TRUST in the Divine—in that invisible, vast unknown—takes mind-boggling effort at times. Sometimes it feels as if prayer is nothing more than talking to ourselves. And sometimes, especially when we are in the midst of fear or despair, it's easy to wonder, *Where is God now? Where is the help I have been asking for?*

I get that—believe me, I do.

There is no reason at all why you should trust me when I tell you that prayer is power; that every prayer is heard and answered; and that everything we do and say is known. I'm not sure *I* would believe me, had I not had the experiences I've had. But I have indeed experienced enough profound and holy moments of divine intimacy—just a few seconds each—that I know it is true. As Teresa of Ávila once wrote, "When God gets into the walls of your soul for just a second, that's enough for a lifetime." She was right.

So that is my prayer for you. May you experience the power of prayer for yourself. May you be bathed in grace, every step of your life. And may God get into the walls of *your* soul—even for a second. Just a second will be enough for the rest of your life. I promise.

Index of Graces

The following index will help you find an appropriate prayer when you need an infusion of a certain grace. Prayers are listed by number.

Acknowledgments

IT IS ALWAYS A PLEASURE TO EXTEND LOVE and gratitude to the people in your life—and heart—who have supported you in countless ways during the rigorous task of writing a book. That is especially true when the author had so many doubts about whether to write this book in the first place. I owe a debt of gratitude to my dear and forever friend and business partner, David Smith, for his endless faith in the power of prayers—and in the need to share these prayers with others—and in his dedication to serving others through our work at Caroline Myss Education (CMED). His heart has become a true servant of the Divine. I am very blessed to have a close circle of loving friends and family members who have always been my garden of oak trees in this life. That support was especially appreciated during the years of incubation for this book, when I relied upon the encouraging words of those I love and trust to go forward. Though words of gratitude are inadequate to truly express all that I feel, it is with deep love and appreciation that I thank my mother, my brother Ed, and my nieces and nephews Rachel, Sarah, Allison and Angela, Joe, and Eddie, who never fail to fill my life with joy. That same love and gratitude is in endless supply in my heart for my wonderful family of beloved friends: Cristina Carlino, Ellen Gunter, Andrew Harvey, Bronwyn Boyle, Beth Zacher, Joyce Chu, Judith Lalor-Sarkine, Janet Watt, Alice Sullivan, Jim Curtan, Mary Stephany, Jill Angelo, Mary Heidkamp, Robert O'Hotto, Sally Prescott, Charles and Sue Wells, and C. Norman Shealy, M.D., Ph.D., all of whom can even make writer's block endurable. And finally, my thanks lovingly pours out to my longtime friend and spiritual director, Thomas Lavin, Ph.D., who has walked miles on my journey with me. My thanks to every one of you.

I would also like to thank the thousands of students of mine who have requested copies of the prayers I shared during these past years in my workshops. The suggestion to compile a book of prayers first came from people attending my workshops, and from responses sent to me because of a prayer posted online. I doubt I would ever—ever—have considered doing a book on prayer had it not been for so many wonderful people from all over the world asking for copies of prayers that touched their hearts. I have included all those prayers in this book in their honor.

The support of a publishing team is everything. Every writer knows a brilliant editor combined with a successful publishing house are the two greatest blessings she can have—and I was blessed with both. My thanks, appreciation, and deep admiration pours out to my editor, Kelly Notaras, for her genius and dedication. I am so grateful for all your incredible talent, patience, and that sharp editorial eye that truly makes a great editor. And thank you, Patty Gift, always, for your ever-present, hovering editorial guidance.

My thanks also to Reid Tracy and the Hay House family for years of support. I especially appreciate their patience, among so many other fine qualities. They truly embody the soul of Louise Hay, one of the most inspiring human beings I have ever had the pleasure of meeting.

About Caroline Myss

CAROLINE MYSS is a five-time *New York Times* bestselling author. She is the co-founder of CMED (Caroline Myss Education Institute) and has taught workshops on consciousness, healing, energy medicine and mystical theology around the world for 35 years. Caroline offers a number of courses on her website: **www. myss.com**

Hay House Titles of Related Interest

YOU CAN HEAL YOUR LIFE, the movie,
starring Louise Hay & Friends
(available as an online streaming video)
www.hayhouse.co.uk/louise-movie

THE SHIFT, the movie,
starring Dr. Wayne W. Dyer
(available as an online streaming video)
www.hayhouse.co.uk/the-shift-movie

***

ALREADY HERE:
A Doctor Discovers the Truth about Heaven,
by Leo Galland, M.D.

FINDING LOVE EVERYWHERE:
67 ½ Wisdom Poems and Meditations, by Robert Holden

MARY MAGDALENE REVEALED:
The First Apostle, Her Feminist Gospel & the Christianity
We Haven't Tried Yet, by Meggan Watterson

MORE BEAUTIFUL THAN BEFORE:
How Suffering Transforms Us,
by Steve Leder

All of the above are available at www.hayhouse.co.uk

***

'The gateways to wisdom and knowledge
are always open.'

Louise Hay